BACK SEA

Back Seat Driver
Memories from the End of Empire

OLIVER KNOWLES

Penn Press Publishers Ltd

First published in Great Britain by
Pen Press Publishers Ltd
25 Eastern Place
Brighton
BN2 1GJ

ISBN 978-1-906710-08-8

Printed and bound in UK by Cpod, Trowbridge, Wiltshire

A catalogue record of this book is available from
the British Library

Cover design by Jacqueline Abromeit
Copy-edited and typeset by Oxford Publishing Services, Oxford

List of Illustrations

Contents

Acronyms and Abbreviations

ADS	assistant director of supplies
ANC	African National Congress
BCMS	Bible Churchmen's Missionary Society
BOR	British other rank
CD&W	colonial development and welfare
CDA	community development assistant
CEPGL	*Communauté économique des pays des Grands Lacs* (Economic Community of the Great Lakes Countries)
CID	Criminal Investigation Department
DADS	deputy assistant director of supplies
DC	district commissioner
DDST	deputy director supplies and transport
DSIR	Department of Scientific and Industrial Research
EAC	East African Community
EAR&H	East African Railways and Harbours
ECA	Economic Commission for Africa
ECOWAS	Economic Community of West African States
EEC	European Economic Community

GDP	gross domestic product
GOC	General Officer Commanding
HM	His/Her Majesty
ICS	Indian Civil Service
JCR	Junior Common Room
KADU	Kenya African Democratic Union
KANU	Kenya African National Union
KAR	King's African Rifles
KBC	Kenya Broadcasting Corporation
KUR&H	Kenya and Uganda Railways and Harbours
L/Cpl	lance-corporal
LMS	London, Midland and Scottish (now defunct railway line)
LSE	London School of Economics and Political Science
MIT	Massachusetts Institute for Technology
NAAFI	Navy, Army and Air Force Institutes
NCO	non-commissioned officer
OC	Officer Commanding
ODI	Overseas Development Institute
OECD	Organization for Economic Cooperation and Development
OTC	Officer Training Corps
OCTU	Officer Cadet Training Unit
OTS	Officers' Training School
OU	Oxford University
P&T	Posts and Telegraphs
POW	prisoner of war

PPE	Philosophy, Politics and Economics
PT	physical training
PWD	Public Works Department
RAF	Royal Air Force
RCD	Regional Commission for Development
RIASC	Royal Indian Army Service Corps
RNVR	Royal Naval Volunteer Reserve
SOAS	School of Oriental and African Studies
UNCTAD	UN Conference on Trade and Development
UNDP	United Nations Development Programme
USAID	United States Agency for International Development
VD	venereal disease
VE	victory in Europe
WAAF	Women's Auxiliary Air Force
YWCA	Young Women's Christian Association

Glossary

banda	hut
boma	government administrative station
darshan	audience hall
heshima	respect
kabaka	king (Buganda)
Kaya	traditional holy meeting places
mganga	witch doctor
mshenzi	uncivilized person
morho	council
ngoma	literally 'drum', but refers to dancing, drumming and singing
nullah	dried-up river bed
pombe	palm wine
shamba	small farm
shauri	affair
Sindano ya kuzaa	injection of birth (penicillin)
syce	groom
tonga	pony trap

Author's Preface

THESE MEMOIRS were mostly written in the 1980s shortly after I retired from working for the United Nations. They were originally written for the benefit of my sons and grandchildren and I had no intention of publishing them. I did, however, place a copy in the Oriel College library where the Cambridge historian Dr John Lonsdale recently read them. He was highly complimentary about them and generously offered to write a foreword should they be published.

My wife June, who writes under her maiden name, Elizabeth Watkins, and is a biographer with four published biographies to her name, has helped me redraft my early years, and some of the chapters that concern our married life have been expanded. My original letters to my mother from India and Burma are now in the Imperial War Museum.

I have no pretentions to being an author; in fact I was trained to write reports like a civil servant. I was, however, fortunate to have been born during the latter years of the British Empire and to have such wonderful and interesting opportunities to travel, and to serve both the British Empire and the United Nations. I hope therefore that I have been able to preserve for future generations some idea of what life was like and how countries were governed during that period, for it was an age that will soon be forgotten. It was an Afrikaner, Laurens van der Post, who described the British Empire as the nearest thing the world has seen to a Platonic system of government. I hope that my readers will agree with him.

My grateful thanks are due to Dr Lonsdale and to my wife for their encouragement and their help, and to my editor Selina Cohen and my cover designer Alexa Garside, without all of whom this book would never have appeared.

Foreword by
John Lonsdale

Reading Oliver Knowles's memoirs it is salutary to reflect on how much has changed in one man's lifetime – and how little. Much of this change and continuity is beyond the control of any one man, and in his final pages Oliver acknowledges how much his life has owed to chance. But he also fails to admit how much depends on what one then makes use of the accidental opportunities life has to offer. Beyond his or any other single person's control was the end of the age of European imperialism and its replacement by a plethora of international organizations. Oliver served both Empire and United Nations. Both were seemingly large and impersonal institutions. Nevertheless, the senior UN official who helped to set up the Association of South East Asian Nations in the 1970s had to employ the same personal powers of persuasion within a large and complex negotiating process as did the junior district officer who got a hospital built in colonial Kenya, at Malindi, in the 1950s. These memoirs give many opportunities for the reader to pause and speculate both on how far individuals can affect the course of events larger than their own lives and on what frustrates such efforts, even when – perhaps particularly when – such efforts seem to be transparently for some common good.

Much of what Oliver Knowles recalls in this rather modestly titled book may come as a shock, particularly to younger readers. The past, even the relatively recent past, really is a different country. Not many Britons nowadays reach the rank of lieutenant-colonel by their mid-twenties, at the price of being able to recall four friends from school and university killed in war, and a fifth held prisoner-of-war for five years. Nor would many now claim that the experience of being bullied was a good preparation for life – although more would agree on the beneficial effects of cross-country running. It is hard to imagine a student room dependent on a coal-bucket for its heat, still less a student willing to put up with that or thinking nothing of it.

But there were many advantages to being a Briton in the days of empire. To judge by Oliver Knowles's own experience and that of his family, it afforded extraordinary opportunities for upward social mobility to people of talent from modest backgrounds. Then, once one had reached the ranks of the imperial officer-class the 'British world' was set up like a global gentleman's club. Team sports, horse-racing, even a facility to take the home civil-service exam, were available anywhere a British official might find himself. In Oliver's case this ranged from Aldershot to Rangoon in the army, and then from Kisii to Lodwar when in the colonial service in

Kenya – even if it required a bit of administrative ingenuity and cheek to get a swimming pool or squash court in the latter far-flung outpost of empire.

While it was a time of wartime danger and postwar austerity it was also an age when junior British officials – far removed from the harsh strategic choices that dismayed their seniors – could still enjoy the extraordinary confidence that came from seeming to represent a Top Nation. It was even possible when on leave to walk across the Himalayas from India to Tibet. The United Nations scarcely seems to generate the same self-confidence, perhaps because its officials are often so far removed from the public they serve. The UN does everything by aeroplane and international, air-conditioned, hotels. The empire used to make do with camel, donkey, or foot safari between nightly camps under the stars. Some might say that the rot set in with the arrival of the Land Rover in the 1950s. It separated the motorized official from his pedestrian public. But four-wheel drive, one discovers here, was also a boon to a family life that was otherwise too often benighted upcountry in imperial mud. The self-indulgent Fulham farmer is an altogether later phenomenon.

Within the global narrative of empire and post-imperial international agencies there was, we discover, still room for personal and family stories to influence history more widely. Oliver's father- and mother-in-law had been influential figures in colonial Kenya. The former, Oscar Watkins, whom Oliver never knew, had met with all the paradoxes of personal dissent within an institutional framework to which he was bound by duty and by pension rights. His personal efforts had been unable to prevent the tens of thousands of African porters in the army's Carrier Corps from suffering terribly in the German East Africa campaign of 1914–18. And the greater his known concern for African welfare the more his career was blighted in colonial Kenya. And yet, as we can read in this memoir, it may be that Watkins's reputation for fairness among Africans caused Jomo Kenyatta, anti-colonial politician before he was a well-disposed President, to put his trust in June, Oliver Knowles's wife, at a particularly tense moment in colonial Kenya's inter-racial relations. [1] His own reputation and experience as a Treasury-trained economist helped Oliver himself to play a formative role in the young Republic of Kenya's young life. Personal relations and individual qualities can never be erased from the grander narratives of history.

That is one of the unchanging truths that emerges from this narrative of rapid and fundamental change. There are other continuities too. One is the colossal strain that service overseas puts on family life, whether that service be for Empire or the United Nations. June Knowles's mother, Olga Watkins, had agonized over 'the awful price of Empire' between the wars, when mothers were parted from young children who went 'home' to be

1 For Watkins's career see June Knowles's biography of her father, writing as Elizabeth Watkins: *Oscar from Africa: The Biography of O. F. Watkins* (London: The Radcliffe Press, 1995).

educated at boarding school.[2] After the Second World
War, when Oliver and June became parents, good education could be found for young Britons overseas,
whether in a colony like Kenya or an international centre
for expatriate civil servants like Geneva. But there was
still a heavy price to pay in constant postings, long leaves
in inadequate lodgings and such tropical diseases as
malaria. On top of that there were the hierarchical
disciplines and narrow social life among officials and
wives at colonial district headquarters, the *boma*, which
the Knowles's found hard to bear. But the stiff etiquette
required also reflected how easy it was, under tropical
conditions, to 'go off the rails'. Even so, it took Swiss
administrative stiffness to deny to June the right to her
own bank account as late as 1969, a difficulty her mother
had encountered as long ago as 1915 in Kenya. Women
continued to pay a high price for their husbands' imperial
or international duty. Samuel Baker, nineteenth-century
English explorer and Egyptian pasha, constantly on the
move, is alleged to have instructed his wife by telegram,
'Pay, pack, and follow.' Official life in the twentieth-
century empire was a bit more respectful of family life
than that. But not much.

It is natural that Oliver Knowles should conclude his
memoirs with reflections on the different ways in which
his two main areas of official service, Africa and east Asia
have subsequently turned out. East Asia has prospered

2. Elizabeth Watkins, *Olga in Kenya: Repressing the Irrepressible*
   (London: Pen Press, 2005) p. 98.

and, with the major exceptions of Vietnam and
Cambodia, has been largely at peace. Africa has in some
respects and in some countries, regressed and Africans
are too often in conflict. There are many possible reasons
for this contrast. Oliver concentrates on two, population
growth and official corruption. These reasons are present
in both Asia and Africa, but he points out some important
differences. He is surely right to conclude that official
probity is more a matter of social and institutional structure than of individual morality. British colonial servants
were kept up to the mark by a strong *esprit de corps* and a
decent pension. African public figures have to measure
up to pressing demands from extended families, unsup-
ported by reliable pay, let alone by a decent pension.
Most people try to meet their obligations. But obligations
vary with circumstances. There is a limit to which
individual qualities can alter the larger picture.

Trinity College, Cambridge

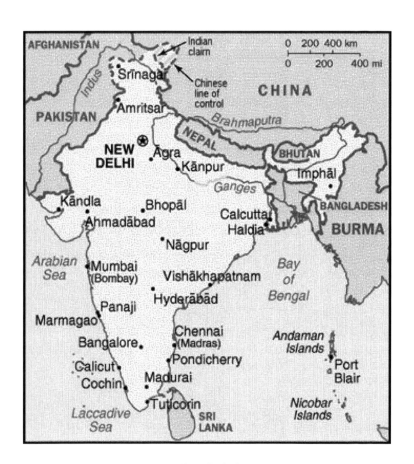

1. South Asia.

1

Early Years

I WAS BORN in Warrington on 23 February 1920 into a professional family, albeit a modest one. My father was a solicitor who, at the age of 37, started to practise on his own. My mother was a year younger than he was and, unusually for those days, was professionally qualified as a pharmacist. They had met 18 years earlier at a tennis club, when they were both very young and sang in the same chapel choir, but they were too poor to get married before 1919; even then it was with some financial help from my grandfather who must have been anxious that his eldest daughter might never marry. My mother always said that those 18 years were very long years indeed.

They came from similar backgrounds. Both families were descended from Yorkshire and Derbyshire hill farmers; both families had names – Knowles and Hill – that denoted this fact. Both were forced to leave the land by the enclosure movement of the late-eighteenth century. Both found the adjustment to wage earning in the industrial revolution a somewhat roller coaster ride. My paternal grandfather was born before 1833, so his birth was not registered. He started work as a wire drawer, near the bottom of the economic pile, and rose to become owner of his own wire mill, at Llantarnan in South Wales, producing barbed wire for the Franco–Prussian war and living in a handsome Victorian villa. He was undercut by the Belgians who introduced a cheaper method of production and scooped the Australian market. He returned, bankrupt, to his native Warrington, where he set up a small workshop making brass bed-steads. It was not very profitable. He had a social conscience and was one of the founders and earliest members of the Warrington Cooperative Society.

My father was born in 1882, not long before his mother died, no doubt exhausted after bearing 14 children, of whom only four survived to adulthood. The eldest of the family, my Aunt Bertha, was then already 20 years old. My father suffered several childhood illnesses, which weakened his health to the extent that he was passed as unfit to serve in the First World War. Aunt Bertha was perforce an extremely economical house-keeper and, right up until her death in 1954, she would cut newspaper into small squares to use instead of toilet paper. My father's diet and medical care no doubt suffered, and there was little money for his education. However, his elder surviving brother, my Uncle Harry, was working in Sheffield selling steel products to Sweden, and sent money home. He eventually became secretary to the Wrought Iron Research Organization and helped with the rationalization of the iron and steel industry in the

1930s. He never married, took early retirement after an illness, and lived with his sister Bertha for the rest of their lives. They moved to live near us, and were *in loco* grandparents. I was very fond of them, and could do no wrong in their eyes, but my mother found Aunt Bertha a rather difficult surrogate mother-in-law. After my own parents, they had the greatest influence on my childhood. Uncle Harry had both the time and patience to teach me many things, from gardening and pruning roses, to typewriting and principles of sound financial investment. He particularly liked insurance companies.

Fate had been kinder to my mother's family. Her grandparents had exchanged farm life in Derbyshire for the ownership of a public house in Cheshire. Unfortunately, the new publican became rather too fond of his products and died while his children were still young. His widow bought a boarding house in Blackpool and sent her son to the Masonic school at Bushey in London, which then provided a good education in stern, almost Dickensian, conditions. Bushey was considered too far from Blackpool for the boy to return home more than once a year. When he left school he was apprenticed to a pharmacist in Scotland Road, Liverpool, a tough and polluted area, where he learnt about the market possibilities of cough mixtures. Once qualified, he moved to another pharmacy in Warrington and not long after this, set up his own pharmacy. He had a good business head and eventually owned six pharmacies in and around Warrington. He invented a new cough mixture, which he called Hills Lung Balsam, which, because it contained tincture of opium, gave one a nice relaxed feeling and sold very well. It can still be bought today in pharmacies, though it no longer contains opium which had to be removed before it could be advertised on television many years later. It is now called Hills Bronchial Balsam.

Grandfather Hill, who believed in the education of women, hoped that his three children, two girls and a boy, would follow him into his business. His eldest girl, my mother, was sent to Manchester University to study pharmacy. She and one other were the first women to attend a pharmacy course, and the men resented their presence to the extent that they would set out to reduce them to tears. She was a shy retiring person, unaware of her own considerable abilities, and begged her father not to make her complete the course. He was adamant and possibly rightly so. When she had taken all the exams in her stride, he employed her in his pharmacies. He paid her the same as he paid his male employees, but banked and then invested the money for her. Over the 15 years that she was to live at home it provided a useful nest egg, and when she was widowed a few months before the start of the Second World War she was well qualified to do her war work in the same pharmacy then owned by her brother Edward.

Edward had wanted to be a farmer, and asked his father if he could study agriculture, but he too complied with his father's wishes and eventually took over the

2. Author with his maternal grandfather, J. S. Hill, 1920.

pharmacy business, though I do not think his heart was in it. It was not until my grandfather tried to make his third child, my aunt Dorothy, also become a pharmacist, that he met his match.

She stood up to him, refused to go to Manchester University, and instead got herself accepted by a physical training establishment in Liverpool – at this time physical training and gymnastics for schoolgirls were becoming very fashionable – and became a PT instructor. She too inherited a good head for business, and eventually became a partner in a private school that became one of Scotland's leading girls' schools. It was unusual for private schools to make money during the slump, particularly at a time when education for girls was still regarded as a luxury rather than a necessity.

Though I was born in Warrington, within a year we moved to the leafy suburb of Latchford Without, then outside Lancashire on the Cheshire side of the Manchester Ship Canal. On removal day my mother pushed my pram for the whole three-mile journey to our new house, which stood behind a neat little front garden, and, across a road, faced the Bridgewater Canal. From an upstairs bedroom, a perfect lookout for a small boy, I could watch cars and barges, steam rollers repairing the road and, in winter, even a horse-drawn icebreaker on the canal. In 1923 my sister was born and I was sent to Aunt Bertha for the day. It is reported that when I returned home and looked down at the dark haired infant in the cradle I was furious, not because she had arrived but because I had been sent away and not allowed to see her birth. Mother must have been sufficiently modern to be as truthful as one can be to a three-year-old about where babies came from.

My father, by nature a literary dilettante, was fond of essayists and had been one of the two founding members

3. Author with his father, 26 September 1920.

of the Warrington Philomathic Society before the First World War. He was also an excellent after-dinner speaker and kept a notebook of funny stories considered suitable for such occasions; a local newspaper voted him 'the second best after-dinner speaker in Warrington ... after the Bishop'.

His office hours fitted in with his dilettante nature, and my mother found them very trying. He would go to his office on the 10.30 a.m. bus, lunch in a café at 3 p.m., and return home at about 9.30 p.m. unless going dancing or to a Masonic evening with my mother. Despite his

4. The author and his sister, *c*.1927.

irregular hours my mother and father were very happy
together and shared many common interests, particularly
ballroom dancing and music, and I have many memories
of them playing duets together on our piano. The

Philomathic Society used also to hold play readings in our house, in which Uncle Harry would participate.

My father's relaxed attitude to catching railway trains reflected his attitude to office hours, and he did not believe in spending time on railway platforms if he could arrive at the last minute. On train journeys he would have us all in a state of nerves by descending at intermediate stops for a cup of tea and rejoining the train at the last possible minute with the cup in his hand. On one occasion he got left behind at Carstairs, and my mother, who was meeting the train in Edinburgh, found only his umbrella, bowler hat and suitcase in the train. When he did take time off from the office he was a good father and knew what small boys liked. A walk to the thatched village sweet shop in Grappenhall to buy Liquorice Allsorts and 'gob stoppers' was a regular event on a Saturday afternoon; and once a year there would be a day outing to the pleasure beaches of Southport or Blackpool.

By nature, my mother was a shy person with a highly developed social conscience and a religious turn of mind. She was very methodical, even if some of her methods were not very labour saving. She suffered from migraines and, at least once a month, she would retire to bed with a siphon of soda water and I would hear her vomiting. Migraines were a characteristic of all the Hills of her generation. It would appear to be a trait inherited from my maternal grandmother. My mother spent a long time in the kitchen, where her approach was that of a pharmacist preparing a prescription. She was almost a compulsive maker of pastry, and I spent much time eating through stacks of mince pies, in which the gluten did me no good at all, as I found when I was many years later diagnosed as a coeliac. Her religious interests largely took the form of good works through Cairo Street Chapel, though she was also interested enough in Unitarianism to become a governor of Manchester College, Oxford, which at that time was a Unitarian theological college.

So, I was fortunate to grow up surrounded by loving supportive adults, all clever enough to value education though not always rich enough to be able to afford it. In this family circle everyone set an example of honest hard work. Industrial England in the 1930s could be a depressing place, with long queues of unemployed people outside the labour exchanges, bare-footed children running around the streets and war-threatening dictators strutting about on the continent. As a small boy I listened to Uncle Harry's stories of his business travels to exotic sounding places, and decided that I too would like to travel when I grew up.

CR80

My first encounter with the outside world was of course through school. In all, I went to four schools: Marlfield School in Grappenhall; the Friends School, Penketh, near Warrington; Willaston School, Nantwich; and Mill Hill School, London. I still have a clear memory of my first day at school. I was six yeas old when my mother walked me down Victoria Road to Marlfield School. Two elderly ladies ran it – Miss Parkinson (an Anglican), who was an old friend of my mother's, and Miss Mary McInerny (Roman Catholic). The fees were modest and it was run on a shoestring with remarkable results considering the financial limitations. It was housed in an old Victorian house with a large garden and adjacent field where we played hockey. It offered girls an education up to school certificate level, but took boys only for the kindergarten stage. The house always smelt of the school lunches, stale cabbage and meat stew, and I doubt if a modern school inspector would have passed the buildings.

I was taken into the school morning assembly, where a mistress, Miss Edith Chadwick, was thumping out a hymn on the piano. It was 'There is a green hill far away, without a city wall'. I was placed in Miss Chadwick's class along with two other small boys, Wallace Miln and Frank Berry, with both of whom I remained in contact until after the Second World War.

Wallace was in a Scottish regiment, was taken prisoner of war at St Valery in 1940 and spent most of the war in a German prisoner of war camp. I had a desk in the front row, near the coal fire that burned in winter. I made good progress under Miss Chadwick, who was a kindly and sympathetic teacher, but who committed the cardinal error of making me – a left-hander – write with my right hand.

From Miss Chadwick's class, the following year we

moved up a floor to a Miss Goodey, who was less sympathetic but a reasonably competent teacher; and the year after that we went to Miss Parkinson and the Revd Darwall, vicar of Lower Walton, who taught Latin – and he taught it very well indeed. In one year I learnt enough to carry me through four years of little or no Latin at my next school without being too backward at my third school.

My time at Marlfield was on the whole happy, though getting there and back could pose problems because, half way up Victoria Road, there was a family of larger boys who sometimes laid ambushes for the smaller Marlfieldians going to and from school. The only incident I recall at school was when I fainted from cold when snowballing one winter and this created a certain amount of alarm and concern among the old ladies. They administered a tot of brandy, which I promptly spat out. My mother, needless to say, made a lot of fuss and consulted our general practitioner, Dr Manson, as a result of which for a while I had an obligatory daily rest inflicted on me after lunch.

When I was nine, I was moved from Marlfield and sent as a boarder to the Friends School, Penketh. This was a traumatic experience, of the kind that enabled the British to run a colonial empire. The bullying was bad in the dormitories, and 'Sticky' Naylor, the matron who looked after the younger boys, was either unable to stop it or unwilling to interfere. As a result of the bullying several boys regularly wet their beds and had to be supplied with rubber sheets. I am glad to say I did not have to suffer that indignity. The one happy memory I have of 'Sticky' Naylor is of *The Wind in the Willows*, which she used to read to us every evening before lights were put out and the evening mayhem commenced. Being a Quaker school, the governors and headmaster, 'Sammy' Maltby, took pride in running the school in as plain and simple a way as possible, with no frills. This meant that the catering, in particular, was of a low standard. The teaching was uneven. Language and Latin teaching were very bad, with French being taught with a new-fangled phonetic system I found completely incomprehensible. Maths and the sciences were reasonably well taught, and the music and woodwork were excellent. My happiest memories are of making wooden recorders from bamboo on winter evenings by the fire in the room of the music mistress, Miss Nightingale, and then learning to play them. I also made some progress with piano lessons. Cross-country runs featured regularly in the recreation programme, and I recall many painful afternoons spent running across the mud flats near Fidlers Ferry on the flood plain of the Mersey, which was so polluted that the flats gave off rather vile smells. It was no doubt good training for later African foot safaris in Turkana.

I went on a school outing to Pendle Hill in Lancashire, where George Fox had the vision that inspired him to launch the Quaker movement. On Sunday mornings we would be marched to the Quaker meeting house in Penketh where we would sit in silence rather uncomfortably on wooden benches for an hour, interrupted only by the surreptitious crackle of sweet papers and an occasional spoken intervention from a senior elder 'inspired by the Holy Spirit'. On most Saturday afternoons either my father or mother would come to see me and take me out to tea, which usually consisted of baked beans on toast at a small teashop across the road from the school. After two years I was able to convince my parents that the bullying and the poor food warranted changing my status from a boarder to a dayboy. This involved a 7 a.m. start from home to catch two buses, but even in winter this was preferable to boarding. It must have been difficult for my mother to run a household coordinating my early start with my father's late one, and with my sister leaving midway between us, but a child does not see that.

I went to Willaston School, Nantwich in 1933. It was a small public school with a Unitarian foundation, which a Nantwich tanner had rather inadequately endowed at the beginning of the century. As a result of its financial constraints it had always struggled, and its numbers had never exceeded 60 boys. A new and dynamic young head, Hector Jacks, the youngest son of Dr L. P. Jacks who had been principal of Manchester College Oxford, had replaced its longtime headmaster, Henry Lang-Jones, in 1932. At the time of his appointment Jacks was just 29, which made him the youngest head in the country. There was every sign therefore that the school was about to turn over a new leaf. Introduced by an old boy, Arnold

Chadwick, the nephew of my father's old friend known in the family as the 'poet Chadwick' because of the awful doggerel he wrote on his Christmas cards each year, my father and I went to see the school in Arnold's open Morris car. We liked what we saw and there was a friendly atmosphere about the place that was absent from Penketh. Hector Jacks was what the French would describe as *sympathique* and was obviously full of enthusiasm and ambition for the school.

It was on the whole a happy time. I was not a cricketer, but I spent many pleasant summer afternoons lying on the grass watching school matches. I was not particularly sporty, but the small school numbers required every boy to play his part, and I found a place in the school rugby team and in the swimming team. In the rugby team I was a second row forward who occasionally managed a sneak try from out of a scrum. In the swimming team I swam as the number two in the breast stroke team, after a lanky boy called Jackson Minor, whose long legs always enabled him to beat me. I also became a patrol leader in the Scouts, on which organization Jacks was very keen, and spent some enjoyable field days crawling across the bracken at Doddington Park, the home of Sir Delves Broughton, as well as learning such useful skills as how to light a fire with one match with dry bark, and how to tie a wide variety of knots. My various scouting skills later stood me in good stead both in Burma in the war and on safari in Africa.

The teaching at Willaston was again a little uneven, but fortunately good in the subjects that interested me, particularly French, which an Australian Mr Lavender taught and Latin, which Hector Jacks taught. Maths might have been good if I could have heard the master, 'Buggy' Ross, an oldish man who whistled through a rather droopy moustache and, being slightly deaf, could not keep very good order in class. He was undoubtedly both a good mathematician and a good chess player. 'Pizzy' Whorwell taught the science subjects, but he again could not keep good discipline in class, with the result that his chemistry classes sometimes resembled a mild form of civil disturbance, with a variety of bangs and strange smells emerging. I learnt very little physics but rather more chemistry, and quite a bit about the sex life of axolotyls, of which we had a pair in a tank in the laboratory, and which were the pride and joy of one of the boys, Fleetwood, who later became a curator at the natural history museum in Nairobi.

In a small school one soon knew all the boys and I made a number of good friends, among them Rupert Thackray who played the school organ and who later emigrated to Australia; Philip Heale who later married my sister; Abdulgani Ydlibi, the son of a Syrian cotton broker in Manchester who later moved to Mill Hill with me and was killed in the war as a pilot in the RAF; Ronald Sokell, the son of the Unitarian minister at Warrington, who was also killed in the war when he was shot down over Burma as a navigator in the RAF; Bill Bliss who went up to

Oxford to St Peters Hall and had very aesthetic tastes (his mother was even more aesthetic). I was also an admirer of Ken Longden who regularly hit a century for the school at cricket, usually with a good many sixes, and was also no mean performer as a jazz pianist.

Half terms were memorable occasions spent at the Brine Baths Hotel in Nantwich, a comfortable old-fashioned spa-type of hotel. In my final year I was a school monitor and also unexpectedly managed to win the school chess championship, defeating the previous year's champion, who was unacquainted with the Evans Gambit, which I had mugged up especially for the final. Winning the toss I luckily had the first move so was able to play the gambit. Although Hector Jacks managed to push up the school numbers, it was the period of the 1930s' slump in Britain, and by 1936 the school was being pressed by its bankers. The governors decided reluctantly to pull the carpet from under Jacks and close the school the following year. There was a lot of sadness about this decision, as given more time there is little doubt that Jacks could have pulled the school around.

The closure of the school in 1937 came at a very inconvenient time for me. In view of the impending closure I sat my A levels (then called the Higher School Certificate) rather prematurely in 1937 and failed. Hector Jacks then arranged for me and Ydlibi to go to Mill Hill School in London, where his older brother Maurice Jacks was the headmaster.

Transferring to a new public school at the age of 17,

5. Author as a schoolboy at Mill Hill.

after I had been a monitor at my old school, was an
uncomfortable business; neither Ydlibi nor I fitted into

the accepted hierarchy at our new school. We could obviously not be made to fag as new boys, but in the school tradition we were still new boys. Some uneasy compromises were reached. For Ydlibi it was easier than for me because he was a first-class batsman and made it into the school first cricket eleven in his first summer. With some difficulty I made it into the second rugby fifteen and into the swimming team. I also managed to come out top of the modern sixth form in French, all of which assured me some status, but I never made it as a monitor or a school prefect and was always regarded as an outsider. We were both in School House, which occupied a building that had seen better days and was much in need of redecoration.

Not being a prefect I had to share a study with three other boys, which was not very conducive to good work. I made one good friend at Mill Hill, Anthony Brett-James. He was a patrol leader in the Scouts, but at Mill Hill this was rather looked down upon and regarded as an alternative to the Officer Training Corps (OTC) and the home of pacifists. He was the eldest son of one of the masters, Norman Brett-James, a historian. At the end of my first year at Mill Hill, Maurice Jacks resigned to become director of the department of education at Oxford University. A Dr T. K. Derry replaced him, but after a few years Derry left to join the BBC. I got a good higher certificate in French and Latin from Mill Hill and, with Hector and Maurice Jacks's support, I applied for a place at Oriel College, Oxford. Hector Jacks also managed to arrange a closed exhibition of £50 a year from a fund at Willaston that had survived the closure of the school and had been endowed in memory of an Old Willastonian killed in the First World War. This represented one-sixth of my Oxford budget so was a considerable help, particularly when my father died during my first year at Oxford.

2

Oxford:
The First Two Years

MY PARENTS HAD always hoped that I would make Oxford and I liked the idea. I sat and passed the Oriel College entrance exam at Easter 1938. While going up for the exam I met my first Oxford friend on the platform of Bletchley station – David Gillott of Ampleforth who was sitting the same entrance exam as I was. In those days the best route from the north to Oxford was via Bletchley along a bumbly LMS line that ambled through the Buckinghamshire countryside and a series of small stations with such rustic names as Marsh Gibbon and Poundon. It arrived at the old Oxford LMS station, which later became a tyre and exhaust repair shop until it was built over.

David Gillott was a sincere Catholic and his approach to his faith made a lasting impression on me. Catholics in the college in those days were put under the benevolent eye of Billy Pantin, a bachelor and one of the last Oxford 'characters'. He was a historian and an authority on Oxford history. His rooms were on XV staircase in the

Rhodes block on the third quad, where I also had my first rooms under the care of Cook, the staircase scout, an ex Royal Navy petty officer, who kept a kindly but firm eye over his charges. Billy Pantin was a source of amusement to him, and one afternoon after the war when Pantin was out, Cook beckoned to me to look inside his rooms. The floor of the sitting room was covered with piles of books, into which Pantin would dive for references when giving tutorials. In his bedroom his bed was surrounded by about fifty pairs of old shoes in a neat line. He apparently had never thrown a pair away.

College life was rather more luxurious before than after the war, even though the total cost of the university was only £300 per annum. With a scout and a 'bedder' for each staircase, breakfast, lunch and tea were served in rooms by the scout, who also lit the coal fire in the morning, while the bedder made the bed, emptied the washbasin and cleaned the rooms. Every set of rooms consisted of a sitting room and one or two small bedrooms, depending on whether the set of rooms were single or shared. Socially, the college reflected the divisions in society, with a small group from one or two fashionable schools who did a minimum of work, drank a lot of beer, played games and hunted or beagled. The bulk of undergraduates were from public schools, solid middle-class men who would get a reasonable second or third class in their finals. There was also a fair number from grant-aided grammar schools, who were at the top end intellectually and provided many of the firsts.

Comprehensive schools did not exist, but Oriel had a number of undergraduates from the USA and the Commonwealth, largely as a result of the Rhodes connection. The public school atmosphere tended to lead to cliques. I attached myself to a Stowe–Rugby group that included Henry Palca from Rugby, with whom I remained a close friend until he died in the late 1980s, his friend John Badenoch who later became a distinguished doctor and was knighted, Miles Weatherall, son of a former principal of Manchester College, who also became a distinguished academic, Graham Cheale, who was killed in the war, and David Gillott, who was also killed in the war and gained the George Cross.

At the end of my first term my father died suddenly and my financial situation looked precarious. Provost Ross was very sympathetic and understanding but that did not solve the cash problem, which was eventually solved by kind uncles, one from each side of my family.

My first year was the last year of peace before the onset of the Second World War and the end of a social epoch. It was the done thing to play plenty of games, and I managed to get into the college rugby team and into the rowing third eight (known as the Rugger Eight) where I did not distinguish myself, catching a crab just below Donnington Bridge on the first day of Eights week. We were bumped on four days out of six. Rowing in winter was a chilly occupation, but the best part was the return to one's rooms and a hot bath followed by anchovy toast by the room fire. I also played squash and took up change-ringing with the Oxford University bell-ringing society. This met on Wednesday evenings in the tower of New College, where we practised with muted bells, or in Mary Magdalene church, where we were not muted. On Saturday afternoons in summer the more expert ringers would cycle out to one of the Oxfordshire villages and ring a peal of Grandsire Doubles or Plain Bob Minor on the bells of the village church. The Oriel cricket club also ran a second team, the Oriel Outcasts, which used to go out and play village cricket, as well as take on the women's colleges. I only once played for the Outcasts because I was pretty hopeless at cricket, and that was in a match against St Hildas when we all had to play left-handed.

I had decided to read jurisprudence because my father and mother hoped I would go into my father's practice as a solicitor. Oriel had no law tutors, so I was sent to Dr Hanbury at Lincoln for Roman law (which involved reading Gaius and Justinian in the original Latin texts) and land law, and to Humphrey Waldock at Brasenose College for criminal law. Long hours were spent in the Codrington Library at All Souls looking up cases. More interesting were the criminal law lectures of Professor Stallybrass, the principal of Brasenose, who had a reputation for lingering over the details of all cases of sexual offences. He was a bachelor who imbibed more alcohol than was good for him and who was eventually killed falling out of a train on his way back from a dinner in London.

Sir David Ross, the provost of Oriel, who was a moral philosopher and author of *The Right and the Good*, had a rather formidable wife and four daughters. One of the ordeals for new undergraduates was to go to Lady Ross's Sunday afternoon tea parties. Sunday afternoon tea parties were an Oxford tradition and I also went to Maurice Jack's house on Shotover Hill for a Sunday tea after he had become director of the education department at Oxford. The vice-provost of Oriel was Marcus Niebuhr Tod, another philosopher, of whom the little epigram ran:

My name is Marcus Niebuhr Tod,
I have the autograph of God,
I am the sole epigraphist
With the Almighty on his list.

The senior tutor was Eric Hargreaves, a roly-poly man who became a temporary civil servant during the war and had something to do with the shoe rationing scheme. He taught me economics after the war.

After Chamberlain's Munich visit in August 1938 it was obvious that sooner or later there would be a war, so I joined the 'gunner' branch of the university Officer Training Corps. I chose the gunners because free driving instruction was included in the course and I could not drive. Sergeant-Major Slatter of the OTC consequently spent a number of rather hair-raising moments giving me driving instruction on the new Oxford bypass.

When war broke out in 1939, as the possessor of a gunner Cert. B, I was eligible to go to an officer training school. However, the leisurely pace of the war in its early months did not require a general call-up and I was advised to carry on at the university until needed, while continuing my OCTU training. The next year, 1940, saw an acceleration of the war culminating in the British army's disastrous withdrawal from France at Dunkirk, as a result of which the army lost most of its guns and there was little demand for potential gunnery officers. However, I realized that I would soon be called up and, at the end of the summer term, I handed over my Woolworth's kettle, china and a few other oddments to my old college scout Cook and left Oxford, wondering if I would ever come back.

Towards the end of the summer vacation of 1940 I received an offer of a cadetship in the Indian Army, which was then being expanded. This appealed to my sense of the romantic and to my pocket, for the pay was generous, so I signed up. I was told to stand by and await mobilization instructions.

I did not therefore go back to Oxford in the autumn but stayed at home. I filled in my time by learning to touch-type on Uncle Harry's typewriter and, to earn some pocket money, tutoring a young girl for the school certificate resit at Christmas, for she had failed in the summer. I am glad to say that under my tuition she passed her exams. While doing this I received a letter from the Colonial Office, whose application form for the colonial service I had completed the previous year through the Oxford University appointments board, asking if I would be interested to join the Royal West African Frontier Force, with a promise of a guaranteed job in West Africa in the colonial service at the end of the war, an assurance that my war service would count for my colonial pension, and an offer to get me released from any other military obligations. However, I was not at that time interested in West Africa, and the Indian Army sounded much more interesting. So I declined the offer and awaited my call-up for India.

3

India and Burma

J UST BEFORE Christmas 1940 and shortly after heavy air raids on London, Liverpool and other cities, I received an instruction to proceed to Willems Barracks Aldershot to join the Royal Scots as a cadet in a draft to India, and on 21 December 1940 I wrote home to my mother:

I arrived yesterday afternoon and found people still drifting in. There are a few from Oxford, one or two of whom I know by sight – the last term's President of the OU Conservative party is in my platoon. Equipment was issued today. We are attached to the Royal Scots whose uniform has a sort of 'Tam o'shanter' instead of a forage cap. Equipment issued includes a Gillette razor and a needle and cotton. Auntie Bertha will be pleased to know that I have received two pairs of long johns. We are kept busy, at least time has been pretty full so far, though a lot of it is wasted. Reveille is at 6.30. There is a NAAFI canteen in the barracks where food and cleaning stuff can be purchased at amazingly cheap prices, though the tea has a curious flavour and the buns are rather rubbery. I managed to buy a roll of toilet paper in Aldershot today. It is very necessary as toilet paper is only issued to officers.

We have a very decent sergeant for our platoon. He is from the Tanks. The worst sergeants to be under are those from the Guards, and their commands sound like puppy dogs barking. I think I must have the biggest head in the whole battalion. However, I have just managed to get into a large 7 ½ inch cap.

It did not take long to get into the ways of the army and a week later I wrote:

The L/Cpl in immediate charge of the sick ward is a sanitary inspector in civil life and enjoyed regaling us yesterday with some of the old sweats dodges for getting into hospital when there is to be a draft. These include rubbing your stomach with a rough brush to produce imitation shingles, or smoking a cigarette soaked in iodine to send up your pulse. He is incidentally a glider pilot.

I was on cookhouse fatigue today. Tell Uncle Harry that an army cook is not a desirable job. Today I managed to get out of the way when there was any washing up to do. I mostly cut bread in a machine and put butter through a slicer. I also washed out the mustard pots. Judging by the accumulation inside them this must have been rather an original idea.

As we would have to sail to India in a convoy, and German submarines were at this time very active, it was a matter of some importance to obfuscate sailing dates and whereabouts as far as possible. After a few days in Aldershot barracks, square bashing and being issued with uniforms and equipment, we entrained for a mystery destination. This turned out the following morning to be Gourock, where we embarked on *The Highland Chieftain*, a ship that in peacetime worked the frozen meat trade from the Argentine and Uruguay. A large convoy was obviously forming in the Clyde, and after several days in the river we set sail, proceeding in a northwesterly direction. Our route was a very roundabout one, passing near Iceland, and then down the Canadian and American coasts, before turning sharply east again and heading for Freetown in Sierra Leone. By this time two of the ships in our convoy, an old Greek passenger boat called the *Nea Hellas* and a free French liner the *Pasteur*, were having sporadic engine troubles and kept dropping back, delaying the whole convoy and causing a dilution of our naval escort.

In Freetown we were not allowed ashore and spent two days in the middle of the large, beautiful harbour staring at the red-roofed houses on the shore before sailing for the Cape. By this time the officer cadets, who made up half the ships' passengers, were getting a bit restive – the OC troops was reported to be sleeping with a revolver under his pillow. We slept in hammocks in what was obviously an old frozen meat hold, and accommodation was pretty cramped. Food was poor, although a few enterprising old Etonians managed to bribe the chef who prepared the food for the ship's officers to let them have the leftovers from the officers' table.

We filled our time aboard with ship drills, Urdu lessons and lectures on the Indian Army from a few old hands who were conducting the draft. We also published a ship's magazine, the *J11*, which was the convoy code number for the ship. When we had nothing else to do we played bridge. I think I played more rubbers of bridge on that voyage than in the rest of my life combined, and I became quite a good exponent of the Culbertson system of the forcing two and the 4–5 no trumps. The main luxury of the voyage was when our daily fruit ration to prevent scurvy was issued. The apples tasted particularly delicious.

At Cape Town our convoy of more than twenty ships divided into two parts, one staying in Cape Town for bunkering and revictualling, the other going to Durban. We went to Durban. On our first day in Durban I had the misfortune to be selected for guard duty on the 'Glasshouse' (the ship's guardroom and prison) and so missed the best hospitality offers, which those going ashore on the first day snapped up. On the second day there was not much choice left, but we did manage to get a free lunch from some kind hosts and in the evening, with a couple of friends, we stood ourselves to a memorable dinner at the King Edward Hotel. No bottle of wine has since tasted as good as the bottle of white wine we drank that evening with our dinner, neither have fresh pineapples ever tasted better.

The Highland Chieftain had in the meantime developed mechanical faults and the Indian Army cadets were transferred to the Windsor Castle, one of the Union Castle Line's intermediate vessels in which we found we had been promoted to cabins. Rejoined by the Cape Town contingent the convoy continued north, skirting Madagascar. German spies in Durban had no doubt reported our departure, so it was hardly surprising when, as we neared Mombasa, there were reports of a surface raider in the vicinity. However, by this time the Australian cruiser Sydney had joined the escort and steamed off to tackle the raider. This turned out to be an Italian and not a German ship and, at the approach of the Sydney, it turned tail and ran for Mogadishu in Italian Somaliland, where it remained until the capitulation of Somaliland to our army advancing from Kenya in late 1941. At Mombasa we were again not allowed ashore and I had the frustrating experience of spending my twenty-first birthday sitting on the deck of the Windsor Castle peeling potatoes and gazing at the roofs of Kilindini.

After Mombasa our convoy split, the greater part continuing north to Suez where the desert army was being reinforced to prevent Rommel's advances. We did not know that it would be nearly two years before he was held at the battle of Alamain, only 40 miles from Alexandria. The *Windsor Castle*, which had a fair turn of speed, was then authorized to break convoy and zig-zagged towards Bombay with all possible speed.

It would have been unwise to let 500 cadets loose in Bombay after several weeks at sea, so we were hastily marched to a troop train that headed south for Bangalore. Our train appeared to have some priority, for we passed many trains in sidings on the way, including several trainloads of happy Italian POWs who had been captured in the Western Desert and were heading for POW camps just north of Bangalore. They appeared delighted to have been taken prisoner and to have been given the opportunity to visit India.

Our first 24 hours in Bangalore were like those of Cinderella arriving at the ball. We marched up from the station late at night still clad in our rather dirty Royal Scots cadet uniforms and went to bed. We woke in the morning to find a personal servant (bearer) standing by each bed with morning tea and toast, and a polished Sam Brown belt and brown boots. From that moment we had no cause to complain about our conditions and lived in Kiplingesque luxury. Our training was a curious mixture of ancient and modern, of comfortable and uncomfortable. At the uncomfortable end we spent many hours in the hot sun crawling across Agram Plain (known in the OTS as 'Agony Plain') on military exercises.

At the more enjoyable end we used to go for riding

6. Cadets at OTS, Bangalore, 1941. Author on left.

lessons to the Mysore Lancers, where after some initial
bareback instruction in the ring to strengthen our thigh
muscles, we were mounted on chargers and used to
gallop cross-country in groups rather like scenes from a
film of Skinner's Horse in *The Indian Mutiny* or the *The
Lives of a Bengal Lancer*. The enjoyment for me was one
day interrupted when my horse caught a hoof in an ant-
bear hole, stumbled and sent me flying over its head.
Fortunately, the thick pith helmet I was wearing absorbed
most of the shock of the fall and I was able to remount
immediately. At weekends I found we could sail at the
Bangalore sailing club at Hesarghatta, where there was
always a demand for crews and where I spent several
pleasurable weekends.

After three months at the OTS our draft received their

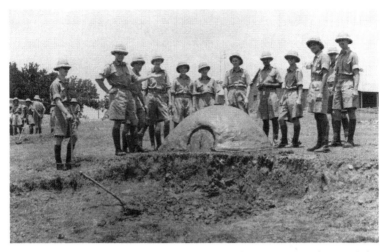

7. Making a field oven at RIASC School, Kakul, 1941. Author on left.

commissions as second lieutenants and we were allowed to go on short leave before proceeding either to regiments or to specialized training schools.

I spent a very enjoyable week walking, riding across the downs, playing squash and absorbing good food in the cool of the Nilgiri Hills at Ootacamund before proceeding to the Royal Indian Army Service Corps (RIASC) school at Kakul near Abbottabad in the Hazara District of the North West Frontier. It was a long train journey with a weekend break in Bombay, but this time we travelled in air-conditioned comfort. Travelling by train was then, and probably still is, one of the best ways to see India and Indians, and I began to get the feel of the country.

Alan Spedding, a chartered accountant from Bolton, accompanied me on the train. When we arrived in Bombay he had the bright idea of looking up 'chartered

8. RIASC School, Kakul, 1941. Author is next to Kenneth Law (in light shirt) in centre of back row.

accountants' in the phone book and enquiring whether there was an institute in the area and if a journal was published. Having selected a firm called Sharp & Tannan in Baroda Buildings, we went inside and asked for Mr Sharp.

We only had to wait a few minutes while Mr Sharp, a Scotsman who had been in Bombay for 20 years, interviewed a Parsee who wanted his son articled. We soon learnt that he was a member of the Bombay Legislative Assembly and was obviously a man of influence. He offered us the use of his car and chauffeur for the afternoon, and invited us to lunch the following day at the Royal Bombay Yacht Club, which had an exclusive membership and reportedly the best cuisine in western India. We were in Bombay for three days during which we also dined with him at the Willingdon Club; for most of this time he extended us the use of his car and chauffeur, thus enabling us to swim at the Breach Kandy swimming pool. With his wife and children in England and having been unable to take leave in England for two years, he lived in a suite at the yacht club. I think he enjoyed entertaining us, for his parting words were 'Come and see me, boys, whenever you are in Bombay.'

Abbottabad was a typical British military cantonment town and the RIASC school was pleasantly situated a few miles out of town at the foot of some low hills in a garden-like environment. I spent a very agreeable three months there learning the intricacies of supply and transport staff work, swimming in the pool and playing squash. My only sad recollection of that time is of one of my friends being killed by a blow from his opponent's squash racquet while playing squash. At Kakul I shared a room with a very pleasant Indian officer, Kenneth O. Law, a Christian whose father was the principal of the Christian theological college near Agra. He had a charming wife and small baby with whom he used to spend the weekends in Abbottabad. I believe he remained in the Indian Army after the war and rose to the rank of major-general.

On leaving Kakul I was posted to the seventh Indian division, then the reserve division for the North West Frontier, in case the Germans made a breakthrough at Stalingrad and raced through the Caucasus and Afghanistan. My first station was to a brigade at Batrasi camp in the North West Frontier Province where I found myself as the officer commanding a small supply section,

a posting that earned me promotion to captain. In
October, at the end of the hot weather, we moved from
Batrasi down to Attock Fort, which Moghul emperors had
built. It was a very solid construction that stood guard
over the bridge where the main Delhi–Peshawar road
crosses the River Indus. In days gone by it must have
been an important bastion against frontier tribesmen, but
with the pushing forward of the frontier to the Khyber
Pass, it had little military importance. It did, however,
provide a convenient centre for divisional headquarters
and there were a number of peacetime amenities such as
tennis courts and a house suitable for the GOC, who
nevertheless complained that the kennels were not good
enough for his hounds (he used to hunt or beagle nearly
every day).

My military duties were not too arduous and could for
the most part be carried out in the morning. They usually
involved spending several hours in a hot stuffy office with
the thermometer well over 100° Fahrenheit – it could go
as high as 130° Fahrenheit at Attock in the summer –
before returning to the mess for a curry lunch and siesta.
This would be followed in the late afternoon by a game of
tennis and a cold beer. In addition to my normal duties I
was made air raid precautions officer for the fort. This
was largely a sinecure because the likelihood of the
Germans bombing us was virtually nil, but it at least gave
me a pretext to inspect the dungeons of the fort, where I
found Emperor Akhbar's torture instruments still in
position and apparently untouched since Moghul days.

While at Attock I was sent on a camouflage course at the Camouflage School in Poona where I had my first flight in a De Havilland Rapide to inspect our camouflage handiwork from the air. I had hardly returned to Attock when I received an urgent posting to go to Wah to join a brigade sailing for Rangoon to defend South Burma against the Japanese advance from Malaysia. I had already embarked on a ship at Calcutta when a telegram arrived requiring me to give evidence at the court martial of an officer who had been fiddling the mess funds. In retrospect, this was one of the luckiest things to happen to me in my life, for the brigade I should have joined was trapped on the wrong side of a river because the engineers had prematurely demolished a bridge. The officer who replaced me, a Captain Everett whom I later met in Manipur, had to swim the river and spent most of the following weeks retreating, often on foot, the length of Burma. He left me his bicycle, which I was delighted to be able to return to him in Manipur.

On my return from Calcutta I received an intra-divisional posting to a brigade headquarters at Campbellpur. This was a typical military cantonment, situated in open plains some miles from Attock. Our military life was uneventful, but the open plains afforded some excellent riding country and I used to ride for several miles every morning before breakfast. I had one fall when, riding along a *nullah* (dried up river bed) and rounding a corner, my horse suddenly shied at the sight of a dead camel. The only entertainment in Campbellpur was the cantonment cinema to which I used to go on a bicycle. One evening while at the cinema it began to rain heavily – an unusual experience for Campbellpur – and returning home I rode straight into a flash flood as I cycled across an Irish bridge in the cantonment. I managed to swim out of the flood and to salvage my bicycle some 50 yards downstream.

While at Campbellpur I was sent on an ammunition recognition course to Rawalpindi arsenal. Unfortunately, the organizers of the course had not been informed that all ammunition had been removed from Rawalpindi and sent to Nowshera. The course could not be held, and I spent a lazy few days in the comfort of Flashman's Hotel, swimming in the pool and buying Persian rugs from the carpet vendors who arrived by *tonga* (pony trap) and laid out their wares on the hotel veranda.

We continued this rather Kiplingesque existence right up until Singapore fell to the Japanese and virtually every-thing changed overnight. I had been planning an agree-able skiing holiday at Gulmarg in Kashmir in early 1942 when our brigade was withdrawn from frontier duties, about-turned and moved by road to Lohardaga in Bihar to join the 14th Indian division. The long drive down the Great North Road was as fascinating and full of history as the train journey north had been by the Frontier Mail. At Lohardaga we were at the end of a narrow 2 foot 6 inch gauge railway that would have delighted any railway buff, but did not help military logistics.

After two weeks in Lohardaga, the brigade was moved

to the Arakan to protect East Bengal from a possible Japanese advance along the coast from Akyab. The strategy at this time was defensive and we had instructions to prepare strong defensive positions with adequate supplies that we could hold even if the Japanese surrounded us. This would deprive them of the possibility of subsisting on captured stores and making a series of flanking movements as they had done in Malaysia and south Burma. Divisional headquarters were in Comilla, and our brigade had the task of holding the important railway junction of Laksam. It was a dismal place full of mosquitoes and smelly 'tanks' of dirty water.

The monsoon was rapidly approaching, however, and it soon became clear that the Japanese advance along the coast would be minimal for the time being. On the other hand, they were making rapid progress up central Burma, where our army was falling back after the fall of Rangoon and the loss of its main supply bases. Emergency supply lines were being opened up as rapidly as possible and bulldozers were hard at work building a road from Manipur state over the border hills and the Shenam Saddle into the Kabaw Valley of Burma. It was meant to link up with a motorable track that came up from Mandalay so that the retreating army could withdraw from Burma with its vehicles, and the thousands of Indian refugees who were walking up from Rangoon could be evacuated. At the time of the fall of Rangoon there were no troops in Manipur other than a battalion of the Assam Rifles, a kind of territorial unit of semi-

Gurkhas; and a protective screen had to be provided as soon as possible for the retreating army and the defence of the Indian frontier in Manipur.

Since all was quiet in the Arakan, our brigade head-quarters and part of the brigade were withdrawn from East Bengal and sent up by rail to Dimapur, which was the railhead for Manipur. After an uneventful rail journey through the tea gardens of Assam we arrived at Dimapur, to find a scene of chaotic activity with the construction of a major army base in the bush. We hastily embarked by lorry for Manipur and arrived at Imphal, the capital, the following morning to find that it had just been bombed. Bodies were lying everywhere. Japanese intelligence had been good, but not quite good enough, and they had just missed our brigade convoy, which had taken longer to arrive from Bengal than might have been expected. We moved straight through Imphal to Palel, where the old road ended. A gash in the hillside indicated where the engineers were constructing the new road up to the Shenam Saddle and down into the Kabaw Valley. While going through Imphal the brigadier instructed me to go to the local treasury and draw a large cash imprest with which to buy any fish, vegetables or fruit that might be available locally. Owing to the administrative chaos and the activities of Subhas Chandra Bose's followers in Bengal, who were interfering with the railway, we were now on half rations, a situation that could not he sustained for long without a loss of efficiency and morale. At the Manipur treasury I found that all the local staff had run away after the bombing and the assistant resident, John Butter, was with Scottish phlegm paying out cash personally. I was next to meet him in Kenya after the war when we both worked in the treasury in Nairobi. He finished a distinguished career as financial secretary to the Sheikh of Abu Dhabi.

The availability of a large cash imprest was to prove an important factor in the months that followed. Cash alone would, however, have been insufficient without the intermediacy of Lance Naik T. Ngulthong Paita, who was I suspect the only Kuki tribesman serving in the Indian army proper, though a number were serving as scouts in Force 136, a group of irregular scouts defending the frontier hills between Manipur and Bengal. Paita had not been with us in Lohardaga, but I had found him in a reinforcement camp in Bengal where I had gone to fill a couple of vacancies. Some intuitive sense – I cannot describe it otherwise – attracted me to him as opposed to many others, and I asked that he be posted to my unit. This proved to be one of the best decisions I ever made. With Paita as chief purchaser we were able to talk to the locals in their own language, and our brigade had an unrivalled success in the purchase of local fish and vegetables. We were officially on half rations for the whole of the 1942 monsoon season, but the availability of a generous supply of fresh food did much to maintain health and morale. I subsequently got a 'Mention in Dispatches' for my work during this period, but it might have been fairer if the award had gone to Paita.

During the monsoon our main enemies were the mud and mosquitoes, not the Japanese who had very extended lines of communication and were suffering from the mud and mosquitoes even more than we were. Shortly after arriving in Palel the cook and sweeper of the brigade mess deserted. They had been upset by the corpses they had seen in Imphal, and then by a Japanese reconnaissance aircraft that had flown low over Palel just after we arrived. A few nights after our arrival they disappeared. We never saw them again though I had a report that they had been seen in a refugee camp in Dimapur mixing with the thousands of refugees who had walked from Burma. The immediate effect of their desertion was that the staff captain and I had to cook the brigadier's breakfast until they could be replaced. This did no harm to anyone, except perhaps to the brigadier's digestion.

Soon after our arrival in Palel, a divisional HQ arrived and 23rd Indian division was formed of two brigades that alternately moved into the Kabaw Valley and rested in Manipur. There was not much fighting apart from the occasional skirmish between reconnaissance parties, in one of which a Warrington friend of mine, Derek McConnell, the adjutant to a Mahratta battalion, was killed. But we had a real problem with the mud and rain. Most of the stragglers from the retreating army in Burma had by now passed through our lines, but several thousand Indian refugees were still arriving, in the last stages of exhaustion after having walked most of the length of Burma. With little to eat, malaria and dysentery were taking their toll and they began to drop by the roadside like flies. There were some harrowing scenes, but there was little we could do to help other than squeeze some of the worst cases into our returning supply trucks. The retreating army mules also suffered badly and my tent, which was pitched forward of the Shenam Saddle, overlooked a gorge we had christened 'Dead Mule Gulch'. As the monsoon gathered force the rain got worse and I can recall one spell of 80 hours when it rained heavily without stopping. At such times little things could do a lot for morale and a daily rum ration was prescribed for all in the advance brigade. I can still recall 40 years later my pleasure at finding that someone had sent us a case of Palethorpe's sausages instead of the American pork and soya links, which, while no doubt nutritious, tasted rather like cotton wool and were universally hated.

Our division stayed in the forward area for the whole of the monsoon season of 1942, with numbers gradually being depleted by malaria. At one time a battalion of the 19th Hyderabad regiment, which should have had a battalion strength of more than 500 men, was down to fewer than 100, of whom a large proportion were officers. Soldiers from the drier areas of India were less able to tolerate the rain than the Gurkhas and the British, and their anti-malarial drill was also less disciplined. Our mules were in their element and played a vital role in maintaining our forward positions. An elephant company, improvised from the Bombay Burma Trading Company's timber-hauling elephants, had walked out with the retreating army. Now it played an important role in maintaining communications and supplies in hill areas to the south of us. Of less use was a camel company some military genius had moved from the North West Frontier. Camels do the splits in mud and are quite useless. They were back loaded as soon as possible.

I had one attack of malaria, which hit me suddenly one morning in Palel after breakfast. I was whisked down to the field ambulance from where I was sent to the field hospital in Imphal. Before I was able to return to duty I was kept in Imphal for nearly three months, first in hospital and then convalescing with the 4/5th Mahrattas battalion, whose adjutant was a friend of mine and which was resting from frontline duties.

I remained with the brigade until the end of the rains, but was then posted back for a senior officers' course with a view to further promotion. This I duly passed and, after a short break for some leave, which I spent in Rajputana, I was posted as DADS (deputy assistant director of supplies) with the rank of major, to 33rd Indian corps, which was then forming in South India in preparation for a possible amphibian landing in Malaysia in 1943.

Changes were taking place in the top command and overall operational planning was under review. The success of Wingate's Long Range Penetration Group had shown that we had at last learnt to beat the Japanese at their own game. For a while our somewhat uneventful training in South India continued. Corps HQ was located at Jalarpet, a railway junction on the Madras–Bangalore railway line. We carried out a number of not very demanding field exercises. On one of these, where my allotted duties were to site a water point for the brigade, I found myself in the fascinating old temple town of Tiruvannamalai, which might have been a stage set for an episode from Abbé Dubois's *Hindu Manners, Customs and Ceremonies*. At the time of my visit it was where Maharishi Sri Ramana, a Hindu religious leader with a number of European disciples, whom the writer Paul Brunton had made famous, had his ashram. Having sited the water point I was able to spend an hour or so sitting in his audience hall (*darshan*) listening and observing. It was a fascinating experience for a young man.

Life in Jalarpet was unexciting. All there was to enliven the officers' mess of an evening were a few singsongs lubricated with tots of Parry's Madras gin, which tasted rather like enamel paint, or, if you were lucky, of Solan whisky, made in the Himalayas with mountain spring water and not a bad substitute for Scotch. For exercise we rode the army horses in the countryside. Our local food contractor for fresh supplies was Dr Abdulla. His main activity was to run a nursing home with letterheads that read: 'THE HIGHEST AIM MAN CAN ATTAIN IS TRIUMPH OVER HUMAN PAIN.' While at Jalarpet I had three very enjoyable spells of local leave, two at Ootacumund in the Nilgiri Hills, and one at Cannanore on the Malabar Coast, from where I cycled up the coast to the French enclave of Telicherry.

In the first part of 1943 the HQ of 33 Corps was disbanded and I was posted to HQ 11 army group then being

formed in Delhi under General Giffard to take charge of
active operations in Burma from Indian Army HQ. I was
put in charge of the Corps HQ baggage party, which was
sent by slow passenger train to Delhi, which took six days
to reach. On the last night when we stopped at Agra my
compartment was burgled and I lost my wallet and camera.

The military tempo was at first leisurely. There was an
advanced HQ in New Delhi, and a rear HQ in Old Delhi. I
was in the rear HQ housed in the old government
secretariat building with newly constructed lines behind
it for the staff. With a room to myself, it was comparatively luxurious and I spent an enjoyable few weeks
there. In my spare time I cycled round Delhi as far as
Tughlaquabad, absorbing chunks of Moghul history and
reading up on it in the *Oxford History of India*.

In October 1943 Mountbatten was appointed supreme
commander in Southeast Asia and things began to
change. He made a point, wherever possible, to meet all
staff officers personally and very soon all officers in both
advanced and rear HQs were being lined up – on
consecutive days – to shake hands with the great man. By
some administrative quirk I was listed for introduction in
both groups so decided to go both times and see what
would happen. On the second round Mountbatten, who
had a remarkable memory for faces, said with a smile, 'I
think you appeared yesterday.'

With Mountbatten's arrival, planning of an advance
was stepped up. However, the Japanese forestalled us. We
were aware that something was in the wind, but I think

the planners thought that Wingate's activities behind the Japanese lines might deter them from attacking. In early 1944 the Japanese began a major advance into India, expecting to get considerable support from Subhas Chandra Bose and his fifth column 'Indian National Army', and believing that once they had encircled our forward positions there would be little to stop them advancing into India.

We were caught out both on timing and on the main thrust of the Japanese attack. When the Japanese began to advance in the Arakan our immediate reserves were moved to support 15th Corps in the Arakan under General Christison. Then the Japanese began an advance on the Manipur front with a flanking movement that cut the Manipur Road behind 4 Corps, and began an advance on Kohima that was only lightly defended. It became clear that the Arakan advance was only a feint and that the main attack was being launched against our main base at Dimapur. General Giffard had been wrong-footed and we were in a very dangerous situation, with a whole army corps surrounded and dependent on air supplies, and with our main base threatened. To protect Dimapur and force open the road again, the 2nd division, a British division, was available in India, but could not be moved rapidly because of poor communications. Apart from an improvised defence force at Kohima composed mainly of BORs and Gurkhas from the convalescent camp there under the camp commandant's command, there was not much to stop the Japanese capturing the Dimapur base. Fortunately, this small force dug in gallantly in a position on top of a hill around the district commissioner's tennis court and hung on for several days. This prevented any advance by the Japanese down the road, and gave the 2nd division time to move into position and cover the Dimapur base.

With a whole army corps now surrounded in Manipur and dependent on air supplies, a major air supply operation had to be mounted. Mountbatten secured the loan of a number of transport aircraft from the Americans, which were taken off the China airlift, and six officers, of whom I was one, were flown from Delhi to Imphal to reinforce the staff in HQ 4 Corps. We were taken there in a Dakota flown by a young Canadian pilot who took great delight in skimming as low as possible over the hilltops of Assam, and who touched down on the grass airstrip at Kanglatongbi in Manipur with heavy monsoon clouds ominously gathering above. The rain was obviously so near and the airstrip so temporary that the pilot kept his engines running and took off immediately we had disembarked. We had just been collected by a truck when the monsoon rains began.

The airlift worked surprisingly well and we were able to maintain supplies and rations at a higher level than we had enjoyed in 1942. The corps was by now in a strong defensive laager, facing outwards onto the foothills surrounding the Manipur valley and, though the Japanese probed, it was too strong a position for them to penetrate. We now had control of the air and suffered only one or two hit-and-run air raids. With extended lines of communications and poor supplies, the Japanese were at the limit of their advance and it became obvious that it was only a matter of time before we should be pushing them back. I occupied my time in corps HQ with air supply loading tables and logistics, and attending the briefing conferences that took place each morning. These usually rather dull affairs were occasionally enlivened by 'Elephant Bill' Williams, who had a sense of the dramatic and would enter the conference *banda* through a window, wearing a cloak and looking like Batman. His elephant company, which he had formed from the Bombay Burma Trading Company's logging elephants, provided our only overland link via the Silchar trail, which was impassible to vehicles.

SECRET MOVEMENT ORDER DATED 21 MARCH 1944 FOR
STAFF OFFICERS AND CLERKS TO FLY INTO IMPHAL TO
REINFORCE HQ4 CORPS FOR THE DURATION OF THE SIEGE
OF IMPHAL

- -

I.C.M.

SECRET

Subject: Moves
To: Q Maint

I.   The following party of Officers and BORs
will move from DELHI to IMPHAL by air on 23 Mar 44
for attachment to H.Q. 4 Corps:

Lt. Col Hughes   )
Major Tobin   ) From GHQ(I) Simla
Major Brookes
Major Knowles
Major Pigott   From Special Force
Major Gray   From GHQ(I)

Capt. Bennett   )
S/Sjt. A.G. Coleman   ) From Main H.Q.
Sjt R.G. Owen   )   II Army Group
Pte. H. G. Bromley   )

Two Q Clerks   To be detailed by
                                          Rear HQ II Army Gp

2.   Aircraft leaves Willingdon Airport 0700
hrs 23 Mar and is due to arrive IMPHAL the same
evening.

3.   Transport Q Maint will arrange transport
to pick up S/Sjt A.G. Coleman and Pte H.G. Bromley at
Racecourse Camp at 0615 hrs on 23 Mar and thence to
South Avenue Camp to pick up Capt. Bennett 0630
hrs.

4.   Baggage: Officers   80 lbs
                      BORS   60 lbs
5.   Haversack rations will be taken by all
ranks.

6.   Duration of absence, approximately 2
months.

          Address: H.Q. 4 Corps
                     c/o 6 Adv Base P.O.
                     INDIA
No. 50707/Bd3
Main HQ II Army Gp.
21 Mar 44
                                             Lt. Col
                                             S.D. 3

          Copy to   G(Ops)
                     R.A.
                     R.E.

The Manipur road remained cut for three months
until the 2nd division pushed through to bring about a
reunion with 4 Corps in late June, and during these
months I was kept very busy. We had an occasional air
raid when our anti-aircraft guns went into action, but

for the most part little happened by way of fighting. The Japanese attacks on our laager were feeble and, with heavy monsoon rain falling for most of the time, there was not much scope for military action. By way of relaxation in Imphal, the Maharajah of Manipur's internationally famous dance troupe put on occasional performances, after one of which a certain commanding officer's lilo was reputed to have been sent for repairs, but for most of us entertainment did not go beyond an evening singsong in the officer's mess. My mess was particularly favoured in this respect, for someone had 'liberated' a Salvation Army harmonium that provided a tuneful accompaniment.

With the reopening of the road I was no longer required in 4 Corps and was posted back to Delhi in July. After my spell of duty in Imphal I was given some local leave and spent it at Gulmarg in Kashmir with Philip Heale. Our contractor-run officers mess was not, however, very hygienic and shortly after my return I contracted jaundice. Nevertheless, I felt amply compensated by a three-week convalescent leave during which I went sailing at Naini Tal in the Himalayan foothills.

I did not stay there long because in November 1944 army group HQ was moved to Barrackpore near Calcutta in preparation for the 14th Army's advance into Burma under General Slim. Mountbatten failed to get resources allocated for an amphibious attack on either Rangoon or Malaysia, but it was clear that our army now had superiority over the Japanese who were suffering badly

from malaria, and had incurred heavy casualties in both
Manipur and the Arakan, where 15th Corps had also
gone into a laager position and held firm. The
opportunity for a counterattack was too good to miss. It
was decided that 4 Corps would go back into Burma at
least as far as Mandalay to reopen the road to China and
relieve the pressure on General Chiang Kai Chek. A small
amphibious landing was also planned at Akyab in
conjunction with an advance by 15th Corps.

In Barrackpore I was occupied mainly with airlift plans
and staff table calculations. In Calcutta I was fortunately
able to purchase several small Marchant calculators,
which one worked by turning a handle. Using these
enabled Army Group HQ and 14th Army HQ in Comilla
to revolutionize the speed of calculating staff tables and
to eliminate a battery of Indian army clerks.

Military activities left me with a certain amount of free
time. Barrackpore was only an army cantonment a few
miles upstream from Calcutta on the Hooghli and, apart
from a cinema, it had little to offer by way of entertainment, but there was a regular bus service into
Calcutta when we had a free day. On a Saturday
afternoon the races provided both entertainment and an
opulent contrast to the poverty and dirt in most of
Calcutta. On a weekday there was tea at Fleury &
Trinka's Swiss teashop, or dinner at the 300 Club, of
which army officers were made honorary members, or at
Spence's Hotel, which also had a billiard room, or the
Somerset Maugham-style Grand Hotel. In Barrackpore I

had an old HMV gramophone I had bought in Delhi, and Calcutta was a good place in which to buy records because there was an HMV record manufacturing plant at Dum Dum near Calcutta. However, Calcutta was a sad place and one could not be unaffected by the poverty, by the many poor people with nowhere to sleep or live except on the pavements, in the temples or in the Howrah railway station. The problems seemed so insoluble that I was glad to be only a passer-by and to leave the problems to others.

When I did not go into Calcutta on my days off I would get on my bicycle and ride north along the Hooghli to Chandernagore. This town was a French colony, a wonderful anachronism and relic of the days of Clive and Dupleix. It was a sleepy place with crumbling old houses and a languidly waving French tricolour. However, French standards of cuisine still lingered and its gastronomic possibilities far surpassed those of Barrackpore – no army cook could have produced such omelettes.

While I was in Barrackpore I managed a short leave to Shillong, the capital of Assam. From Shillong I visited Cherrapunji, which has the highest recorded rainfall in the world and a self-emptying rain gauge. Cherrapunji had once been a British army cantonment, but the wet climate was found so depressing and the suicide rate so high that the cantonment had been closed. Since the army's departure the recorded rainfall had somewhat diminished. Visual observation suggested to me that there has been little diminution in rainfall, and it seems likely that the rain gauge had been topped up regularly by beer drinking Tommies on their way home to barracks.

From Shillong I visited Margaret Barr in the Khasi Hills. Margaret was a rarity – a Unitarian missionary – who, as a Cambridge graduate, had gone to Calcutta to work with the Brahmo Samaj. She had then learnt of the existence of an indigenous Unitarian church in the Khasi Hills that had broken away from the Methodists and she had seen opportunities for women's education. She had learnt the Khasi language and had established a remarkable rapport not only with the Khasis, a hill tribe, but also with the government and provincial authorities. When independence came, this stood her in good stead and she remained when other missionaries left, even-tually dying in India, though not before she had visited us in Nairobi in the 1960s. I went to Shillong with my future brother-in-law Philip Heale, who was then a signals officer with an anti-aircraft brigade in Chittagong. I think she enjoyed showing us around. She was both determined and energetic, and we walked many miles over the hills visiting schools and small churches.

Slim's advance went remarkably well and in March 1945 he recaptured Mandalay. It was then decided to take a gamble and try to reach Rangoon before the monsoon broke in May. Meanwhile, Christison had recaptured Akyab and was preparing to move down the coast in a series of small amphibious hops. The Japanese withdrew ahead of the advancing 14th Army; even the expected

9. Author and Philip Heale, Shillong, Assam, 1943.

defence of Rangoon failed to materialize, and a small amphibious landing, timed to effect a pincer movement with the army advancing from the north, encountered no opposition. We won the gamble and reoccupied Rangoon just a few hours before the beginning of the 1945 monsoon.

After we had regained Rangoon it was necessary to establish new supply lines and to regroup the armies. A decision was made to pull out the 14th Army and many of its units, both to rest them and to prepare them for further operations in Southeast Asia. A new HQ, 12th Army, was formed in Rangoon to carry out mopping up operations on the 40,000 Japanese troops now surrounded in Burma, and I was posted to the new HQ located in the university buildings near the Kokine Lake. The fall of Rangoon had almost coincided with VE day in Europe and it was clearly only a matter of time before the Japanese would be defeated and the war would end. However, we did not underestimate their tenacity and we anticipated a prolonged last stage. The arrival of the atom bomb and surrender of the Emperor of Japan fortunately shortened this period.

After VE day in Europe the tension relaxed considerably and some priorities changed. Home leave to England began to be possible and the army in Burma was able to make itself more comfortable. A high priority was given to reopening the Mandalay brewery and it was soon producing beer again. It was less successful in producing rum. A rather vicious looking concoction was sent to the government chemist in Calcutta for analysis and the result was sent to me in a rather incomprehensible chemical formula. So I cabled 'Is this drinkable?' To which the reply came 'Quite drinkable, but not rum.'

In Rangoon the engineers turned to building sailing boats and soon we had a fleet of 'Fireflies' with which to inaugurate a sailing club on the Kokine Lake. I spent many agreeable hours sailing and racing in the year that followed. The Rangoon racecourse, where we had a supply base, also received attention and, with a little careful planning, it was possible to combine both the supply and racing functions.

Not long after arriving in Rangoon I was promoted to

lieutenant-colonel and appointed assistant director of supplies for the 12th Army. This was quite a responsibility for a young man of 24, and a military rank I had never expected to attain. As ADS I was responsible to the deputy director of supplies and transport for feeding the army in Burma. I realized that good supporting staff were vital and that my deputy, though a friendly Irishman and a good jockey, was not up to the job. Flying to Akyab shortly after my arrival in Rangoon I met Ronald Montgomery. I realized that Ronald was the kind of intelligent, reliable and unflappable assistant I needed and, by pulling strings, I arranged for his promotion and posting to Rangoon. It was an excellent partnership and we remain in contact 60 years later. Ronald is an Ulsterman and a nephew of Alexander Fleming, the discoverer of penicillin. Like me he later became a Catholic, in his case as a result of marrying a charming French wife.

With our supply base in the racecourse I began to take an interest in racing and bought a racing pony. It and its jockey had spent the war pulling a tonga (a pony trap) to avoid being commandeered for military duties by the Japanese. It was not exactly a star performer, but neither were most of the other ponies and much depended on the handicapper. Unfortunately, just before I bought it, it had won a race and moved up to top weight in its division. It never won again, at least not when I owned it, but I had the consolation that my jockey could usually tell me which horse would win any race other than the one in which he was running.

Being an owner carried important spin-off benefits, including the right to a box at the races. This greatly increased my social leverage, which was of some importance if one wanted to find a dancing partner. The officers' club had a good band and put on a dance every evening, but suitable partners were in short supply and competition keen. Having acquired a box, I arranged with Eric Hall, a friend who was the army catering adviser, to organize a lunch party in my box one Saturday afternoon before the races. I did not lack dancing partners after that, though diaries had to be carefully prepared to prevent overlapping. Mistakes occasionally occurred and I remember one occasion when a friend, Mary Ryder, had triple-dated three lieutenant-colonels on the same evening. However, she carried off the occasion with aplomb and considerable tact.

In August 1945 the atom bombs were dropped on Hiroshima and Nagasaki and the Emperor of Japan ordered his armies to surrender. The formal surrender of forces in the Southeast Asia Command took place in Singapore in September. Thereafter, our primary concerns were to repatriate prisoners of war, set up civilian administrations, and plan the rundown and demobilization of our armies. In line with the new image, 12th Army was converted into Burma Command.

Demobilization was on a points system and based on the principle of first in first out. As I had not donned uniform until the end of 1940 I could not expect to be released until the middle of 1946. As military duties were diminishing and amenities increasing, we had rather a pleasant time, with plenty of sailing, dancing and local leaves. My first leave once rail communications had been restored consisted of a week in Maymo, the summer capital above Mandalay. I then tried to visit Ankor Wat in Cambodia on one of the regular supply flights, but this never materialized and it was another 25 years, when working for the UN, before I was able to visit Cambodia.

I was more successful at organizing a visit to Tibet in early 1946 when I travelled to Calcutta on a returning supply flight and took the train to Kalimpong. In Kalimpong I stayed at the Himalayan Hotel, which David Macdonald, the former British trade agent in Yatung and Gyantse and friend of the Dalai Lama, then owned. Macdonald was Anglo-Tibetan, his father being a Scottish general who accompanied Younghusband to Lhasa in 1902 and his mother a Tibetan lady of high family. His contacts with Tibet were unique. Because of his friendship with the Dalai Lama the government of India used him to contact the new young Dalai Lama in the 1930s; he greeted him as 'my old friend' and carried on the conversation from where he had left off with the last Dalai Lama. Macdonald briefed me on what arrangements to make and how to set about making them, as well as on how to behave in Tibet.

I went by bus to Darjeeling and after a couple of days obtained a permit from the resident commissioner to travel along the Tibetan trade route as far as Gyantse. I then returned to Kalimpong and set about hiring a

10. Setting out for Tibet from Kalimpong, March 1946.

muleteer with three mules. I also hired a cook and bought provisions for a month. These included packets of English tea biscuits, which Macdonald assured me were always acceptable presents in monasteries, as well as a supply of silk scarves, the customary wrapping for ceremonial presents.

In another two days I was ready and set out for the Jelep La pass, travelling via the Swiss mission at Pedong where I was able to augment my provisions with a large Gruyere cheese. I was already in Buddhist territory, and little water wheels to which prayers were attached could be seen revolving in some of the streams. The scenery was magnificent and on the second day I began to climb rapidly. In one morning I climbed from 9000 to 12,000 feet above sea level, passing through a verdant forest of rhododendrons and orchids. At 12,000 feet I was above the forest and ran into a blizzard. I was still clad in my tropical khaki drill clothing and the cold began to make me feel faint. Fortunately, I was not far from the rest house where I planned to spend the night, and I was able to get warm before the cold affected me too badly.

The next day we climbed the Jelap La pass at about 16,000 feet. It was March and the pass was still covered in snow. The bodies of several porters who had obviously been trapped and perished in a blizzard in the winter were lying in the snow; the bodies would no doubt be removed when the snow disappeared. Having crossed the pass we were in Tibet and the Chumbi Valley lay ahead.

We descended fairly rapidly to Yatung, a small settlement and trading post nestling in a pretty valley through which a stream bubbled and gurgled. Yatung is about 10,000 feet above sea level and the next day we climbed out of the valley onto the Tibetan plateau at an altitude of about 17,000 feet. As we crossed a rather bleak plain we could see the mountains of Bhutan on our right and the snow covered peak of Chomolhari.

In the evening we arrived at one of the most forlorn and dirty towns I have ever seen. It was Phari Dzong, which appeared to consist of a number of piles of stone and mud traversed by dirty muddy streets. It was the seat of the local magistrates, the Dzongpens, and Macdonald had advised me to call on them formally both to pay my compliments and to report my presence. There was also a

11. Officers' mess HQ Burma Command in university buildings,
1946. Author seated second from right.

Yellow Hat monastery to visit. By the time I arrived I had a splitting headache from the altitude and my exertions of the day, and thankfully went straight to the rest house.

However, I remembered Macdonald's advice and before retiring sent my cook off with two packets of biscuits, each wrapped in a silk scarf, one for the magistrates and one for the abbot of the monastery. He duly returned with, as courtesy required, presents of rancid butter and very old eggs, which, when cracked to make an omelette, emitted a powerful odour. The next day I visited the monastery, met the abbot and was shown the holy books; I also called on the Dzongpens who received me courteously. As my Nepalese cook was acting as interpreter I only hope the courtesies were adequately returned.

At Phari I had to decide whether to continue over the plains and visit Gyantse, or to turn west and go over the Nathu La pass into Sikkim. As organizing my trip had taken longer than expected, I risked being absent without leave if I went as far as Gyantse and did not want to blot my copybook just before demobilization. The route between Phari and Gyantse also sounded rather dull and uninteresting. I therefore decided to go into Sikkim and the next day set out for the Nathu La. I spent the night *en route* in a rest house reputed to be haunted, but did not see or hear any ghosts.

After crossing the Nathu La I came upon a recently-constructed motorable track and followed this down to Gangtok, the capital of Sikkim, a pleasant verdant little town with a comfortable old-fashioned hotel. I paid off my cook and muleteer in Gangtok and, after a couple of nights there, returned by bus to Kalimpong and to the Himalayan Hotel. I thanked David Macdonald for all his help and through him bought a Tibetan *tangka* as a souvenir of my visit. Macdonald lived to a ripe old age and many years later when he launched an appeal through *The Times* to help Tibetan refugees I sent him a donation from Kenya.

Back in Rangoon the problems of civil government began to press on us. We had a plague of rats and the army sent for a professional rat catcher who set a series of traps in the city, with a number in the vicinity of the large

12. David Macdonald and his daughters at Himalayan Hotel,
Kalinpong, 1946.

Shwe Dagon pagoda. Unfortunately, taking any form of
life is contrary to Buddhist precepts, so the monks would
release the rats from the traps during the night and the
campaign was not a great success. Theft of military stores
also became a big problem in a society of many shortages.
Much ingenuity was used for this purpose.

The pipeline to the RAF airfield at Mingladon was

found to have had a number of holes drilled into the underside, in which plugs had been fitted so that petrol cans could be filled from them. Army jeeps began to disappear when left unguarded and a Chinese gang was discovered that could strip a Jeep down to its component parts in half an hour. These were then sold on the black market and sometimes even made their way up to China.

In August 1946 my release was agreed and I sailed for home on a troopship from Rangoon through the Suez Canal.

4

Ex-Service Oxford

I LANDED IN England at Tilbury at the end of August 1946. I had met on the boat a rather amusing Anglo-Indian, George Fleury, who had been a lieutenant-colonel in the civil affairs department in Burma and who was emigrating to Brazil to start what he hoped would be an emigration programme to Brazil for Anglo-Indians. We decided to spend a couple of days in London before going up to Yorkshire for demobilization. Hotel accommodation was difficult but I had read that the celebrated Rosa Lewis (reputedly an ex-mistress of King Edward VII) who owned the Cavendish Hotel in Jermyn Street never turned away anyone in uniform. So we went to the Cavendish, found Rosa sitting in a large wicker chair in the entrance hall and persuaded her to find us a room. The hotel had suffered from the bombing of London and the room leaked badly, but it was a room. We did a little sightseeing and had one evening out at the Lansdowne Club. On leaving the doorman called a taxi for us. I tipped him half a crown (2/6), but he handed it back saying, 'You need this more than me, sir.'

In Yorkshire the paperwork for our release was quickly

completed and we collected our demobilization clothing issue. I said goodbye to George Fleury and next heard from him in São Paulo in Brazil. I went home to Cheshire for two or three weeks, bought a second-hand Hillman Minx, and drove down to Oxford on my demob petrol ration. This time I found myself sharing a room with Bill Kendal, the son of a former senior police chief at Scotland Yard. Our room was on the ground floor in the third quad of Oriel and was very cold. Our coal ration was limited and it was almost impossible to keep the room warm in what was to prove one of the coldest winters for many years. It was so cold that the River Cherwell froze for its entire length and I was able to skate from the University Parks up as far as Water Eaton.

On returning to Oxford I decided against continuing with jurisprudence. I felt philosophy, politics and economics (PPE) would be more interesting and also fitted in well with the colonial service Devonshire course programme. To do PPE I needed two years at Oxford, but could only get an ex-serviceman's grant for one year. However, by overlapping the Devonshire course with my second PPE year and choosing PPE subjects that overlapped as far as possible with those of the course, I was able to finance myself for two years.

I had applied to the colonial service before the war and, on my return, revived the application when I failed to pass the foreign service and home civil administrative grade exams in Rangoon. I was accepted for the Devonshire course and the interviewing committee duly

13. Oxford, 1948.

interviewed me and allocated me to Kenya (by the time of the interview I had acquired a personal reason for wanting to go there, which I explained to the committee).

The room I shared with Bill Kendal was next to the

college coal hole and one day Bill spotted that the key of the coal hole had been left in the door. He quickly took an imprint of the key in a cake of soap and sent it to an old lag he had got to know through his father, who had been head of the CID. He duly received a key by post and it fitted perfectly, so we had easy access to the college after 9 p.m. when the college doors closed on the last stroke of Great Tom at Christ Church, and without the alternative of paying a fine or climbing over the walls. We were very restrained in the use of this key and had no problems with the authorities. When we went down Bill sold the key. The purchasers were less careful about their use of this entry and the dean soon found out about it, so the lock was changed. In my second term I shared a room with Peter Wassell, a red-haired giant of a man with whom life was never dull; and in the summer term I managed to obtain a particularly good set of rooms in the college annex overlooking both the High Street and Oriel Street.

During that cold winter, one of the coldest on record, the only really warm places were the university libraries, which received a special fuel ration to keep the books warm and free from damp. They became not only a popular place in which to work, but since there was plenty of hot water in the cloakrooms, the men also started shaving there. The New Bodleian was the PPE students' library. The building had been finished just before the war, but the RAF took it over almost at once and the university had only recently moved its books into it. King George VI came down to open it soon after term started, but the golden key he had been handed failed to work. He was a very shy man and did not know what to do. It was only after he had pulled, pushed and even kicked the door, turned crimson with embarrassment and started stuttering in the way he had, that an official realized what was wrong, so took the key off him and carried it away. In the approximately ten-minute interim before the official reappeared with another key, which opened the door perfectly, the chancellor and other high officials in decorative gowns stood around trying to make reassuring remarks to the King.

Apart from the fuel shortage, food was still strictly rationed and the college food was poor. At one point it got so bad that the JCR held a special meeting to which it invited the dean, the Revd John Collins, who later founded Christian Action, to explain why it was so bad. If one had enough money one could supplement college food by eating out after eating in. The 'British Restaurants', which the government opened during the war and which were still operating, provided the cheapest food, but it was of a poor factory canteen standard and they were only open at lunch time. Since eggs were now no longer rationed, a number of snack bars, of which the Stowaway down a passage off the High Street was the best known, would serve an after-dinner omelette to fill in the gaps. It was rumoured that they made some of the omelettes with hair oil.

It was in the New Bodleian library during that cold

winter that I first met June. She thought I had taken a book she wanted to read from the shelf, Habeler's *Prosperity and Depression*, but the copy I had with me was in fact my own. I liked the look of her, so offered to lend her my copy on condition she returned it the next day. We agreed to meet at the Copper Kettle in the High Street, a coffee shop that belonged to the Oxford cooperative society. From this auspicious start, with the help of my car I was able to make good progress. We met on 11 February and saw each other almost every day for a week, I was intrigued to find that she came from a family that had served the empire overseas for two generations, her grandfather as an army chaplain in India and her father as an administrator in Kenya. I also respected her for having left her family home in Kenya to join up, serving as an officer with the WAAF in both Cairo and Italy under active service conditions. It was difficult to find anywhere to meet. I was sharing rooms and June was not allowed to have a man in her room at all during her first year.

I then found a solution. With petrol being limited I was unable to take June very far or very often in the car, in fact only as far as Brimpton Grange Hotel at Milton Common. This hotel, which the Ashley Courtney guide recommended, put on smart dinner dances on a Saturday evening for which a dinner jacket had to be worn, but there was nowhere we could be alone in Oxford. The only place to talk was in the car, but the paperwork and regulations relating to undergraduate car ownership were formidable. The car had to be kept in a specially licensed garage, to carry a special green light so the proctors (the university police) could recognize it, and be garaged by 10.30 p.m. Alternatively, it could by special arrangement be left in the Randolph Hotel garage up to midnight for an extra payment. I discovered that if I took my MA degree, which I was entitled to do by virtue of the law exams I had passed before joining the army and the six years that had since elapsed, I could be exempted from these rules and from proctorial jurisdiction, and remove the green light. We could then park the car in St Giles, which was blacked out because of the fuel shortage, our time limited only by the cold and absence of heating in my car, and by June having to report in early.

During the Easter vacation June had planned to spend a fortnight in the Lake District where the family of a great friend from her WAAF days, Winifred Laws, had a cottage. The family lived in Staffordshire and June joined them at their home as planned for the journey to Kendal. After Winifred's father had gone ahead to prepare the cottage Winifred was diagnosed with mumps and her mother, on hearing that June had not had mumps, forbade her to go near Winifred. She suggested June join Mr Laws in the Lake District, but realizing it would be bad for her reputation to be alone with a married man on a remote farm, she suggested June invite another friend to stay with her. When June phoned me from the cottage I came up immediately and we had a wonderful week walking on the fells. June did the housekeeping and managed despite the lack of running water, electric light and even a cooking oven.

I knew that June's mother and eldest sister, Pella, were coming from Kenya to visit her in Oxford and, as I mentioned, I had been lucky in the summer term to obtain single occupancy of exceptionally good rooms in the college annex overlooking the High Street. I had also obtained tickets for two commemoration balls and, with support from my 'scout' Eric and his wife, was able to give dinner parties in my rooms before each ball. Olga Watkins had been an elected member of the Kenya Legislative Council for some years and on meeting her I realized that she was an exceptional woman. It was a good summer term and Pella paired off at once with a partner I had found for her for the commemoration balls, whom she eventually married.

June had been selected for an Oxford student delegation organized by Lord Lindsey of Balliol to visit Austrian universities during the following vacation and to re-establish contacts with them. She would then join her mother at her grandmother's old home in the Tyrol. Olga shared ownership of Schloss Matzen with her brother who had been an admiral in the war, so had no difficulty obtaining permits from the French. Austria was then subject to occupation by the Allies, and the Tyrol was in the French zone, so visitors had to obtain special visas from the French. I managed to circumvent that difficulty by joining a student group, and visited the family there. While I was at Matzen I heard I had been accepted for the

Kenya administration and the admiral brought up a bottle of wine to drink to our health.

June had a very cosmopolitan family, with relatives in a number of countries. A few months later I heard with great sadness of the sudden death of her mother, before I had a chance to know her better. I was also sorry I never met her father, Oscar Watkins, who had died in 1943. He had been commandant of the Carrier Corps in the East African campaign against the Germans in the First World War and, as a senior administrator in Kenya, had protected further tribal lands from European settlement. Olga, who represented Europeans in Kiambu in the Legislative Council, had laid the foundation of education for African women. June has written a separate biography of each of them, because although they were a devoted couple their contributions to the development of Kenya were very different.

In my second year after the war I moved into digs, at first in Walton Street where the landlady had a crippled husband and kept a large photo of her Methodist minister in the hall. On Sunday mornings she would turn on her radio full blast when the church service came on so that the students upstairs could benefit. Under university regulations for licensed digs in those days, June was allowed into my room until 11 p.m., at which hour our landlady would call upstairs – '11 o'clock, Mr Knowles.' One evening after June had gone, a colleague in the digs, Tim Wood, came into my room and spoke in a high-pitched voice so that our landlady thought June had not left and came up to do a search. She was perplexed to find only Tim there. Our breakfasts got worse and worse, and one day after some particularly greasy sausages Tim complained to the landlady. She erupted angrily, and accused Tim of being 'the Wood in the nigger pile'. We had all had enough and agreed to look for new digs. I found a room in a rather upper-class house in north Oxford belonging to a professor. His wife, who had three unmarried daughters, gave regular Sunday afternoon tea parties, but otherwise spent much of her time painting and repainting the bathroom furniture. The family were, however, kind and the food was good. The professor seemed to spend most of his time in his study either working on a Greek lexicon or doing *The Times* cross-word. He was, however, forced to surface for the Sunday tea parties.

To dovetail my PPE second year with the Devonshire course, I chose to do two optional papers, one on 'colonial economics' and the other on 'the political structure of the British empire'. My colonial economics tutor was Miss Peter Ady of St Anne's College, an Anglo-Burmese whose brother I had met in Rangoon when he was serving with Force 136 and I was ADS for 12th Army. Peter was also June's tutor and she thought we were so well suited to each other that she gave a party at Musgrave House, the St Anne's headquarters, and introduced us to each other. She had mixed such strong drinks that we both became quarrelsome and cycled home on either side of South Parks Road hurling insults at each other. Peter remained a lifelong friend to us both, but it was a long time before we told her that we had already been engaged for a year at the time of her party.

From the autumn term of 1947 I had to work hard, with both PPE finals and the colonial course exams only two terms away. The main lecturer on colonial economics was Professor S. H. Frankel, a down-to-earth South African who lectured on 'capital' and from whom I learnt more economics than from anyone else in Oxford. His family owned a big South African company called 'Tiger Oats' and many years later I was to find myself, when on my way to Andermatt to pick up our youngest son, Johnny, who had broken a leg skiing, sitting in a dining car opposite a Swiss banker who turned out to be a financial adviser for Tiger Oats. On the British empire my tutor was Frederick Madden, with whom Peter Wassell and I had some lively tutorials. The lecturer was Professor Coupland, who could make imperial history sound very interesting.

At the end of my two years I managed a middle second in PPE and went up to London to do a term at SOAS (the School of Oriental and African Studies) learning Swahili, and at LSE (the London School of Economics) as part of the Devonshire course, before sailing for Kenya to join the Colonial Service. London did not match up to Oxford, but with June still there I had good reason to go down for a number of weekends. June had still another year to complete her degree course, which delayed our marriage until 1949 at St Marks church in Nairobi.

5

Turkana

WHEN I ARRIVED in Kenya I had to confess to the chief native commissioner's personal assistant, who was responsible for our postings, that I neither played cricket nor was very interested in bird-watching. This confession apparently left him with no option but to post me to the northern frontier and I was sent to Turkana. It was thus that I arrived in Lodwar on a contractor's lorry in the middle of a dust storm on a very hot afternoon in March 1949. To get there I had travelled by train for 24 hours from Nairobi to Kitale, which was then a small 'settler' township at an altitude of 6000 feet, before beginning the descent from Kapenguria to the bottom of the Rift Valley at an altitude of about 2000 feet.

After a nine-hour crawl from Kitale over a rough track that passed for a road, a lorry dumped me in the middle of a dusty square outside the district commissioner's office. There I found the DC, Leslie Whitehouse (known as Wouse to his colleagues), looking remarkably cool in such uncomfortable conditions. He welcomed me warmly and walked me down to the district officer's house, a

14. DO's house, Lodwar, 1949.

squat rectangular building with a wide veranda covered with dom palm leaves, and a flat roof on which a wire sleeping cage was perched. He introduced me to my predecessor, Peter Barker, who was busy packing and about to leave to get married, for at this time Lodwar was a bachelor station. Matrimonial imperatives did not permit a lengthy transfer and, within hours, a handover safari had been planned and arrangements made to take on Peter's administrative responsibilities.

On my second day I was sent down to the brickworks with a folding chair, a sun umbrella and instructions to obtain an increase per hour in productivity. It did not take me long to see that the labourers were falling over one another and that the same or higher output could be achieved with fewer of them. I dismissed about one-third of the labour force and the next day left with Peter on a handing-over lorry safari to South Turkana.

We became bogged down in a sand river almost immediately on leaving Lodwar, and I began my initiation into the routines of a Turkana lorry safari. At that time four-wheel drive vehicles had yet to be introduced into Turkana and we travelled with a set of sand mats and a team of willing hands from the tribal police to assist us through the numerous sand rivers. On this occasion I was greatly cheered to see a tribal policeman pushing the driver's cab while standing in the back of the lorry! We quickly freed the lorry and drove on through the heat of the day. Driving in such heat was bad for both the lorry and the passengers, and contrary to normal practice, but Peter was in such a hurry to be away and married that we departed from normal practice. As a result, on this safari I saw the finest collection of mirages I have ever seen in my life.

After several hours of driving we stopped for the night at Kangatet, which at that time consisted of a couple of Somali owned corrugated iron stores standing on the edge of a sand river, on the banks of which were some acacia thorn trees, of the kind nicknamed giraffes' dinner tables. We quickly pitched camp. This consisted of placing a table, chairs, camp beds and folding bath under a thorn tree; tents were rarely used in this dry climate. Our ablutions aroused considerable local interest and we quickly acquired an admiring audience of the local youth. These were followed by a posse of local damsels who, when we had dressed and sat down in our chairs to a welcome glass of beer, danced up to us in waves, and by way of light entertainment began to flick their leather skirts in our faces to see who could be the first to land a

15. Turkana pushing a lorry out of a sand river.

spot of grease on the end of a district officer's nose. Established administrative tradition required that we sat in imperial calm without moving. The administration did not often present such opportunities for good clean fun.

Some months later I revisited Kangatet to meet George and Joy Adamson, not then as famous as they became later, who were escorting a group of Turkana, who had strayed beyond their tribal territory and were embarrassing the administration, back from Isiolo on the other side of Lake Rudolf (now Lake Turkana). The absence of good rains and water to enable them to cross the arid inhospitable terrain around Teleki's volcano at the south end of the lake had seriously delayed their return. Arriving at Kangatet by lorry in the middle of a hot Saturday afternoon, I found that the Isiolo contingent had arrived before me. In the nearest tent I found District Officer Bill Stone, an ex-RAF wing commander who had a patch over one eye. As I had fresh supplies I invited him to eat with me that evening, and sent a similar invitation to the Adamsons, whose tent was pitched a little distance away down the bed of the sand river. Late in the afternoon Bill joined me for a beer and about the same time a little rain fell. As it began to get dark the rain stopped and I saw the Adamsons approaching up the stream bed. I greeted them and introduced myself. Joy looked at Bill Stone and, turning to me, asked, 'Is Mr Stone dining with you?' I replied with some astonishment 'But, of course.' 'In that case,' she replied, 'We cannot dine with you.' And with George still following she walked away. I then learnt from Bill that at the Isiolo club on the Saturday night before their departure the assistant superintendent of police had handed Bill a padlock saying 'For your chastity belt, old boy.' Joy had heard about this, had taken umbrage and for most of the journey they had walked 100 yards apart. I repatriated the Isiolo Turkana without any further incidents.

After my first safari I had to settle down to administrative life in Lodwar, a nondescript little township or *boma* overlooked by low volcanic hills on a rocky outcrop between the Turkwell and Kagwalasi rivers. For most of the year the rivers are dry, flowing only during the short period of the rains. They do, however, contain catfish, which hibernate in muddy balls during the long dry seasons. The fort, a small *beau geste* stone construction

16. Lodwar prison and fort.

housing the prison and with a sentry marching on top of its walls, was the township's centrepiece. From sunrise to sunset the Union Jack flew in the centre of a small nearby square containing the administrative offices and everyone in the *boma* would stand to attention when a bugler, playing the Reveille or Last Post, marked its raising and lowering on the flagpole. The square also contained a war memorial to the 1st Turkana Irregular Company, which had fought against the Italians; it consisted of a small pavilion in which the many visitors with *shauris* or other business could shelter from the sun while waiting to see the district commissioner.

The Italian campaign in fact put Lodwar on the map for the first time and provided the DC with unwanted opportunities for administrative initiative. On one occasion a lone Italian bomber dropped a bomb that set fire to some huts. The DC promptly sent a radio message to Nairobi. It read: 'Lodwar bombed; township on fire; construction of static water tank essential against future raids.' The financial secretary authorized expenditure on air-raid precautionary measures and a static water tank (with a design that was indistinguishable from that of a swimming pool) was constructed. The wartime expansion of the transport fleet required the building of a garage. It was found necessary to buttress the rear wall of the garage with a construction that resembled a squash court. Thus, Lodwar administrators managed to maintain their sanity under difficult conditions.

Administrative 'hard cases' and marginal construction proposals were considerably eased by an account known as the 'goat bag', the revenue of which came from the sale of sheep and goat skins from the animals purchased to feed government employees their meat ration. At that time a goat skin fetched one shilling and a sheep skin six pence, and by tradition the butcher who sold the animals to the administration purchased back the skins, having previously charged the administration a price inclusive of the skins. The DC placed the proceeds from the skins in the 'goat bag', which by tradition the government auditor ignored during his annual visit. Since it was not subject to audit this particular account was, as a matter of honour, always scrupulously maintained to the last cent.

The butcher's activities formed an integral part of tax collection in Turkana, for the only way to collect tax from a tribe of nomads with a subsistence economy is to collect a poll or head tax related to livestock values. Since it was a poor district and the butcher in any case had a limited market for the animals purchased, the tax was fixed at a level to correspond to the value of a small goat or large sheep – at that time six shillings. This was just sufficient to ensure a local meat supply and was in principle payable by all adult males. Headmen were responsible for submitting the names of taxpayers, as well as for submitting recommendations for tax exemption on grounds of poverty. Headmen and district officers had much scope to exercise discretion. The system, however, worked fairly smoothly and the working tax register, divided into various clans and subclans, contained the names of 20,000 taxpayers. Since no census had ever been taken in Turkana, and it was administratively impossible to take one with any degree of accuracy, the tax register provided the only guide to the district's population and formed the basis of all administrative planning. It was an accepted convention that in the periodic Kenya censuses the population of Turkana would be reported as four times the number of registered taxpayers.

In a largely non-monetary economy, cash injections into the economy were required even to collect a six-shilling poll tax. To achieve this, the butcher would accompany the district officers on tax collecting safaris. The butcher would sit at one table buying sheep and goats, while the district officer would sit a few yards away at another table collecting back the same money in poll tax payments. If the butcher ran out of cash he would borrow from the district officer, who would record an advance payment for the purchase of the government meat rations. Money therefore had a high velocity of circulation, but unfortunately a low employment and accelerator effect to stimulate the economy.

Social life in Lodwar was decidedly limited, with a non-Turkana population of three European males who spent much of their time on safari, two Goan clerks, a handful of African interpreters and clerks, two Indian traders with their families, two Somali butchers, and some miscellaneous servants and camp followers. Even a game of squash could be difficult to arrange and the main social activity was gossip over an evening pint of beer bought at wholesale prices through the 'Lodwar Atheneum', an organization that existed solely on paper for the purchase of beer at wholesale prices. A previous DC was reported to have spent his evenings playing with clockwork trains on the flat roof of his house. After dinner he would retire to the roof calling to his servant 'Lete whisky and KUR&H' (Kenya and Uganda Railways and Harbours).

I created a social precedent by bringing in a piano and a wife. Each suffered from the conditions – my piano from the dust storms and silverfish, which invaded the felts of the keys, as well as from white ants, which attacked it from underneath, and June from being a pioneering novelty. As she usually wore slacks the Turkana were inclined to assume she was a man and to address her accordingly. A solicitous provincial commissioner forbade her to go on certain safaris because of the assumed dangers involved. In the household my servants, who were used to a bachelor ménage, viewed her control over the consumption of sugar with some misgiving. The DC adapted nobly to the presence of a wife and organized a dinner party to celebrate her arrival. Our little dog Stumpy accompanied us. Unfortunately, the DC's large green carpet was the closest thing Stumpy had seen to grass for some time and he performed on it.

In Lodwar June attempted to conduct some anthropological research at the township water holes. This usually resulted in a hasty evacuation of livestock from the water hole concerned because it was assumed that she was engaged in counting livestock on behalf of the tax collector. It did, however, result in some interesting conversations. On finding out that June was my only wife, one old lady offered her nubile young daughter as a second wife, which she explained would relieve June of much of the more tedious housework and some of her responsibilities in bed. I found out later that one of my predecessors had taken a local partner while in Lodwar and was still sending her a quarterly remittance. Some years ago a BBC programme, *Sex in the Empire*, suggested this was usual practice. It may have been in former French colonies, but my impression is that most British administrators in outstations led rather lonely bachelor lives. Wouse certainly did.

About this time Wouse, perhaps with Stumpy in mind, decided to launch a programme of loo construction in the *boma* and sited a new long-drop near my veranda. When I suggested that the proposed site might perhaps embarrass my wife, he replied, 'She won't mind, I know her family.'

I assumed this to be a compliment that showed June was now a well accepted member of the community.

By this time I had learnt to respect Wouse's cheerfulness, fairness, integrity, courage and endurance under the difficult conditions in which he had to work. On a shoestring budget and under very frustrating conditions he achieved remarkable results in Turkana over a number of years. A lifetime of service to the Turkana people was fittingly crowned when, in retirement as a Kenya citizen at the age of 84 and still hearing cases in Lodwar as a magistrate, he was promoted to Senior Resident Magistrate. After we left Kenya and at the start of the Mau Mau movement, Jomo Kenyatta was detained there and Wouse protected him from his fellow prisoners' serious bullying and threats. When Kenyatta became president of Kenya, Wouse was often seen at Government House, and the next president, Daniel Arap Moi, awarded him the high honour of Grand Warrior of Kenya – a fitting award to one of Kenya's unsung heroes.

His sense of fairness and integrity had occasional bizarre twists. One day in Lokitaung I received a coded telegram from him via the police radio. Since it was in code I assumed it must relate to a security matter and tried to decode it with the police code, but with no intelligible results. I consulted June who had worked in RAF cyphers in the war and, after some thought, she decided to try the post office code. She handed me the text. It read 'Please find out name of European police officer who knocked down camel with his lorry on Thursday and did not stop.'

The possibility of a bizarre outcome was one of Turkana's attractions. Missions and missionaries were not at that time generally allowed to work in or visit Turkana, for the current philosophy was that too much education might destabilize the Turkana and render them incapable or unwilling to continue to live in their inhospitable country. It was with some surprise therefore that on my last safari in South Turkana, when I was taking a siesta in my tent in the heat of the afternoon, I heard a voice outside saying: 'Prepare to meet thy God!' The voice was followed by the smiling face of a BCMS missionary from the neighbouring district of Baringo.

Making economic progress was an uphill struggle. The two achievements for which Leslie Whitehouse deserves most credit were the commencement of sand river irrigation schemes and the development of the fishing industry in Lake Rudolf. Contrary to popular belief the Turkana were not fish eaters by tradition and, at the time of the Second World War, did not know how to catch fish. On Whitehouse's initiative, an old Luo fisherman called Pangrassio was brought in from Nyanza to teach fishing skills at Ferguson's Gulf. After a slow start the programme was a big success and the time when the Turkana did not eat fish has almost been forgotten.

We had not long finished opening our wedding presents when I was transferred to Lokitaung, about 150 miles further north and near the borders of the Sudan and Ethiopia. Though there were three European police officers and an Indian assistant surgeon, Lokitaung was then a one-man station administratively. The main duties of all concerned were to maintain an administrative presence and to keep a watch on national frontiers. The latter were unsatisfactory because they had been drawn with a ruler on a map in Berlin in the 1890s without regard to local geography or tribal boundaries; national boundaries actually split traditional tribal grazing grounds. British administrators in the Sudan and Kenya alleviated the problem by arranging that Kenya should *de facto* administer an area referred to as the Ilemi Triangle and that the Lokitaung magistrate should be gazetted *ad nominem* both in Khartoum and Nairobi to ensure the legality of his jurisdiction.

Periodic meetings between Kenyan and Sudanese police and administrators were arranged by radio to settle border problems, though transport and radio failures often meant that the planned meetings never took place, and one party or the other would return home after camping fruitlessly for several days at an agreed rendezvous. Sudanese administrators regarded themselves as a caste apart and were nicknamed the 'bog barons'. They felt sartorially superior to the Kenyan administration since they went on home leave every nine months and could get their hair cut in Bond Street. Kenyan administrators had to be content with a pudding basin cut in the Lokitaung *boma*.

Relations with the local Ethiopian administrator were more important in view of the raiding propensities of the Ethiopian border tribe, the Merille, over whom Addis

Ababa exercised a somewhat tenuous control. My Ethiopian counterpart, poor man, seemed to lead an awful life. With no health services he suffered from chronic malaria, as well as other complaints.

He appeared not to receive a regular salary and his remuneration, and that of the handful of soldiers under his control, seemed to depend on his selling a proportion of the cattle he collected by way of tax. To avoid the vagaries of Ethiopian tax collection and obtain the protection of the Kenyan government, a small border tribe called the Dongiro had even volunteered to pay Kenyan poll tax. Their case had so impressed one of my predecessors that on his own initiative he had nearly annexed their territory to Kenya, until the provincial commissioner reminded him that this option was not within his powers.

The Ethiopian government's goodwill was unfortunately not matched by that of the Merille tribe, and the handful of poorly paid soldiers at his disposal did not enable my counterpart to deliver much, particularly stolen cattle, against the will of the Merille. However, we persevered and I tried to help him in small ways from our limited resources. He particularly appreciated the help of our medical service. Our doctor earned much goodwill from the Merille by taking some penicillin to alleviate the effects of a dirty knife at a tribal circumcision ceremony. My counterpart helped me in turn by selling me two riding mules, one for myself and one for June, which we exchanged against a payment in kind of a tent from

17. The DO's mule, Lokitaung, c.1950.

Ahmed's in Nairobi, and a handful of silver Maria Theresa dollars, still the *de facto* currency of trans-border trade, which I obtained from a local trader. The mules became great friends and so attached to one another that even when June did not go on safari with me I had to take them both, and the second one trotted behind.

At the next level in the Ethiopian hierarchy came the Governor-General of Gamu-Gofa. I never met this august gentleman, though not for want of trying. After considerable negotiation we arranged for Dick Turnbull, our provincial commissioner, to meet him for a border parley at a lunch to be held at our border post of Namuruputh. Since the lunch was fixed for a Tuesday, a day of fasting in the Ethiopian Church, we had even arranged a fish menu, to be washed down by a suitable supply of gin. Unfortunately for Kenya – and the gin – the governor-general never turned up and I was left with the heavy responsibility of driving a very happy PC and the DC back to Lokitaung.

We were a few miles out of Namuruputh, in the middle of a plain where oryx still wandered, when the DC recalled that he and the PC should have examined me for my standard Swahili oral examination. He pointed out that if I were not examined before we arrived at the Lokitaung airfield and the PC flew back to Isiolo it would be at least six months before another opportunity might occur. The PC, greatly impressed by this argument, rose to the occasion and threw his hat out of the vehicle saying, 'Nenda lete kofia.' I turned the vehicle in a semi-circle, picked up his hat and handed it to him. 'And what,' he said, 'is the Swahili for gonorrhoea?' With our trans-border medical assistance arrangements having added this word to my vocabulary, I passed my exam with flying colours and claimed the appropriate language allowance.

Life in Lokitaung was always eventful and the Turkana never dull. My predecessor, an ex-RNVR officer, had taken his responsibilities extremely seriously and had insisted on being saluted on every conceivable occasion; even a short walk through the township would involve a series of embarrassing salutes and heel clicks. The oppor-tunities to take the mickey out of a new DO were obviously irresistible. In our first week June and I, who had a bed on a sleeping terrace at the side of the house to avoid the heat inside in the hot weather, were awoken just before dawn by a sharp command of 'eyes right'. It was our camel *syces* who were delivering our daily supply of water to the house. A few days later I was sitting in deep contemplation in our long-drop loo at the bottom of our garden when I realized that in the gorge below a young goatherd was standing smartly at the salute. A tribal policeman I sent to give a message personally to June walked straight into the bathroom, saluted smartly and handed it to her in the bath without blinking an eyelid. I had to modify the saluting instructions.

Snakes also added some variety to life. There was a resident snake in our long-drop, which meant that we had to use it with some circumspection. Snakes were also the main enemies of our turkeys and were prone to steal eggs if precautions were not taken. Once when we were leaving for a week in Nairobi we had a very promising batch of eggs under a broody turkey, so asked our young Turkana house servant Kionga to take special care to ensure that the turkeys were protected from snakes. On our return he greeted us with a pleased smile, saying, 'The eggs are quite safe. I took them away from the turkey every night and placed them in the refrigerator.'

The remoteness of Lokitaung made it a suitable station for the detention of politically embarrassing citizens and, in my time, several leaders of the Somali Youth League were detained there. They were a charming group of old men with whom I had excellent relations once I had established that all complaints should be confined to one

18. DO's house and sleeping *banda*, Lokitaung, 1950.

day a month, which became their *shauri* day. To my surprise, no one ever complained about the drinking water, which had a high concentration of natural Epsom salts. But I did have a lot of complaints about their wives, who were allowed to visit them on a monthly rotation and between whom fair play had to be maintained. For most of the time they seemed to play endless games of whist.

A minor administrative task was to take meteorological readings, for which the East African Meteorological Department offered an honorarium of one shilling a day if the readings were radioed to Nairobi. This activity was normally delegated to the district clerk who received the honorarium for his pains. Our readings were considered important because Lokitaung was the northernmost station in Kenya and on the direct flight route between Nairobi and Khartoum. I was concerned therefore when I received a telegram from Nairobi asking me to recheck all our readings for the previous month. June, who had at one time worked in the meteorological department in Nairobi, offered to do this for me. She discovered that both the maximum and minimum thermometers were out of order and the same temperatures were being reported every day. Even worse, the clerk had not known how to record wind direction and cloud cover. Wind directions had been reported as those to which, and not from which, the wind was blowing, and a constant cloud cover had been reported even when the sky was clear. Fortunately, no accidents had resulted.

Our assistant surgeon did not have a lot of work and was obviously bored. When one of our transport camels was reported as wasting away because a thorn branch was stuck in its gullet and it could not swallow food, I asked him if he could do anything about it. His anatomical knowledge was, he thought, adequate. However, there were two practical problems – to administer anaesthesia and suturing through the camel's hide to sew up the cut he would have to make to remove the branch. I am happy to report that the operation was entirely successful and the camel recovered fully. Suturing was carried out with a gunny bag needle and twine and, in lieu of anaesthesia, thirty strong tribal police held the animal down with ropes.

The same doctor was less successful in treating the

Kenya police and, as a result of their complaints, was posted to another station. Because he departed with alacrity before his replacement arrived, the director of medical services sent a telegram asking me to assume temporary charge of the hospital and medical stores. I was surprised to find that the doctor had been in the habit of storing his dirty crockery in the hospital refrigerator, presumably to avoid the need to wash up and to limit the smell.

The working week in Lokitaung revolved around the arrival of the weekly mail and provision lorry, which, river drifts permitting, would arrive on a Thursday evening and depart on a Friday morning. Most of our office activity was therefore concentrated into a hectic 12 hours during the night between the arrival and departure of the mail. Once the lorry had departed and with fresh supplies available, I could leave on safari, which I tended to do every alternate week.

There were three transport options for safaris – lorry, camel or donkey, all of which could be supplemented by some foot-slogging. The choice depended on the terrain to be covered. If tracks existed and the ground was dry, a lorry safari covered most ground in least time, assuming the lorry did not break down. For Mount Lorienatom in the Ilemi Triangle and for the hills on the Uganda border, donkeys gave maximum mobility, but were slow and had limited carrying capacity. For steady plodding across untracked plains, camels and riding mules were the preferred choice. Sometimes a combination could be used, with camels or donkeys sent ahead to wait at a given rendezvous where the motorable track petered out.

Camel safaris had a quality all their own. This was partly because of the desert terrain and water holes, and partly because the animals had unusual digestive and sexual habits. To function effectively the animals needed several hours in the middle of the day to browse on the acacia thorns and other such camel delicacies. The daily march usually began half an hour before sunrise and continued for no less than three hours until a shady spot could be found to pass the heat of the day. The camels would then be released to browse until mid-afternoon when they would be rounded up and prepared for the evening trek, which would last until dusk. The long midday halts would begin with a late breakfast and finish with an early cup of tea. Between these daily landmarks a little poll tax might be collected if a headman had rounded up some taxpayers; cattle rustlers and other offenders could be dealt with; and medicines could be dispensed and dressings applied. The medicine chest contained mainly aspirin and antimalarial drugs, and my treatments were obviously limited, but they were in considerable demand and gave the taxpayers some visible return for their tax. They were usually alas less appreciative of the law and order services we provided.

These safari duties were not onerous and I had plenty of time at the midday halts for reading. I managed to read several Shakespeare plays and Bertrand Russell's *History of Western Philosophy*. Small pleasures had a disproportionate value on long safaris. Bacon and eggs at the breakfast halt, or a cold beer and a hot bath in my canvas bath while watching the sunset over the desert, did wonders for morale after a day of great heat, flies and perhaps blistered feet. Sunburn was a continuing problem for me and a police inspector at one frontier post claimed to recognize me through his glasses from a distance of several miles because of the redness of my face.

It was a unique experience of which I still retain many memories: of breaking and pitching camps (always pitching upwind of the camels); of many dances of welcome and particularly of the haunting melodies and dances of the elders in the Oropoi Valley; of finding an old woman abandoned on a mountain track by a trickle of water far from any village because her clan had judged her to be a witch; of lorry rendezvous when the lorry did not turn up; and once of a return journey of 150 miles on foot for that reason. In retrospect, it was one of the most formative periods of my life. However, even though it was the first year of our marriage, I would not want to repeat it.

6

Malindi

WHEN I RETURNED from a long safari on the frontier, one that was considered too dangerous for June to accompany me, I found her packing furiously. The bathroom stood bare of everything except her canvas bath; the improvised washstand and storage unit had been returned to its original duty of piano case, and the tropicalized piano had been bolted into it.

'Leaving me already?' I asked.

'You are coming too, to Malindi!'

'Holiday?'

'No, posting. We should have moved last week!' Sudden postings were part of a cadet's life, to introduce him to different parts of the country before he became too attached to one particular tribe.

Lokitaung in Turkana to Malindi on the coast was in terms of mileage one of the longest transfers possible and I looked forward to lodging a mileage claim for over 1000 miles at 1/– a mile. My pleasurable sense of anticipation gradually diminished, however, as the journey progressed.

19. Kenya and surrounding countries.

Our vehicle – an American Ford pick-up that still carried the name 'Wispers Farm' on one of its doors and had originally belonged to my mother-in-law, had been laid up for six months in an open-sided shelter June had constructed in Lokitaung with string and without using a single nail. The mechanical parts had in consequence largely filled with sand from the frequent dust storms, and the tyres had partly perished in the heat. We spent the first part of the journey, undertaken at night to save our tyres from the heat, stopping every twenty or so miles to remove sand from the carburettor and petrol system. Then we started having punctures, six in all. We had two spares but it was hard work. By the time we reached Nairobi I had to buy a new set of tyres, and any potential profit from a mileage claim had disappeared into garage tills before we reached Mombasa.

On the journey we also lost an affectionate cat, which in Lokitaung had become an important member of the family. Between Lodwar and Kitale we stopped by the roadside in Karamoja for the night and opened up our camp beds. In the morning, the cat wandered into the bushes on a mission of nature and never returned. We searched in vain for nearly an hour and then regretfully abandoned hope of finding him. We shall never know if a leopard or other predator had caught him.

When we were on leave in Nairobi from Turkana, a kind friend had given us a lovable little mongrel with Chippendale legs whom we promptly christened 'Stumpy'. On arrival in Malindi he took a great liking to the beach and sea, though he unfortunately developed a habit of barking at elderly Arab gentlemen taking their evening promenades. We lost him also in a few months. He must have been bitten by a tsetse fly during a brief stop at Gede, for he developed trypanosomiasis. Although we were lucky enough to have had him treated by a visiting vet, he developed internal bleeding and gradually wasted away from loss of blood.

My predecessor in Malindi, Mike Power, handed over

20. The 'garage' that June built at Lokitaung, 1950.

to me as soon as possible and we moved into the district officer's flat, which was above the office in a stately old house that the old British East Africa Company, the colonial government's predecessor, had constructed at the turn of the century. No one had in fact bothered to change the district seal since the days of the company and all my official reports were therefore sealed with it.

The building was beautifully situated facing the beach. It was solidly built, with large, cool, high-ceilinged rooms and a roof that harboured a swarm of bats. At the beginning, our rooms smelt permanently of bat droppings and we received periodic complaints from nearby hotels about the smell of bats when the wind blew in their direction. We lived for most of the day and ate all our meals on the wide first-floor veranda, where we could enjoy the cool

21. District Office, Malindi, 1950, with DO's flat above the office.
Building constructed by the old East Africa Company.

sea breeze, for it was usually too hot to sit in comfort in the inside rooms. At the end of a day's work it was a great luxury to be able to go straight out onto the beach to swim and surf.

The hour before sunset, when the setting sun cast shadows over the sea, was always the most pleasant time of day. It was also the time of the evening parade when much of the town's population took to promenading up and down the beach. This could lead to culture clashes because stately old Arab gentlemen, even if they might cast appreciative glances at scantily dressed female tourists, felt it necessary to complain to the DO about such improprieties of dress. Arab urchins wore long striped robes; the women all wore the veil; and the Giriama women, who wore frilly white tutu skirts and nothing else, never ventured onto the beach at parade time, though one frequently met them in the town.

North of the district office was a Muslim cemetery and
behind it were the hotels – first Lawfords, then Brady's
Palm Beach (later to become the Blue Marlin), then the
Sindbad, and finally the Eden Roc, owned by an Irish earl
who disliked the British and was known locally as 'JC'. It
had the best swimming pool in town, but his cavalier
attitude to his guests offset that attraction. The Sindbad
had the best all-round reputation and put on excellent
dinner dances on a Saturday night. Lawfords provided the
best food. The Palm Beach did not seem to do much
business and on the only occasion I ventured to lodge an
official visitor there, he found a mouse's nest in his bed.
P. O'Hara Brady was better at propping up his bar than at
running his hotel.

We spent an interesting, enjoyable and exhausting
year in Malindi. At first, coming from Turkana, we found
conditions so different that the transfer was almost
traumatic. In Turkana we had lived a *Sanders of the River*
existence in an uncomplicated and strictly tribal society.
In Malindi we were plunged into a multiracial society
with complex developmental problems. Apart from the
assistant agricultural officer, a fisheries officer and the
headmaster of the Arab boys' school, I was the sole white
representative of His Imperial British Majesty.

The coast's legal status was a typically British
compromise. I was referred to as the *balozi*, meaning
'consul' in Swahili. Although the Kenya government
paid my Liwali assistant's salary, he was regarded as the
representative of the Sultan of Zanzibar from whom the

Coastal Strip, alias the protectorate as opposed to the Colony of Kenya, was leased for a nominal sum that appeared each year in the treasury vote. This legal fiction that the sultan owned the soil and only leased it to the British government was preserved through the staff of the sultan's flag traditionally being placed in the ground, whereas that of the Union Jack being attached to a building. The presence of an official *kathi* (Muslim judge) whose business was to administer sharia law in all family disputes between Muslims further reinforced the Muslims' special status.

My status as His Majesty's sole administrative representative meant that not only were there certain ceremonial and entertainment functions to be carried out, but I was also a sort of Gilbertian Pooh Bah – district officer, magistrate, ex-officio agent of the public trustee, port officer, keeper of the lighthouse, receiver of wrecks, subdistrict accounting officer, officer in charge of the prison and the detention camp, officer in charge of the tribal police, receiver of stolen ivory, town clerk, chief sanitary inspector, keeper of burial grounds, and custodian generally of law and order and public decency (the latter was no sinecure in a tourist resort with a largely Muslim population). These various roles had to be filled at a time of considerable postwar development and economic expansion.

In the year we spent in Malindi we saw a new hospital sited and built, a piped water supply laid down and installed throughout the township, the groundwork laid for the introduction of a township rating system, and several new boreholes and roads completed. Never in my life have I been so busy either before or since. In the heat of the coast, the pressure of work, combined with the endemic malaria and dysentery from which we were not immune, exhausted both me and June, and it was her health that forced us to ask regretfully for a transfer to a cooler and less demanding post. Yet, we greatly enjoyed both the work and the people and made many friends among all communities; subsequent holiday visits to Malindi were always a great pleasure and an opportunity for reunions with old friends.

As HM's official representative the main social event was the King's Birthday, which occurred within a week of our arrival. On this occasion I had to don my white uniform and solar topi, and formally inspect the tribal police, after which a cocktail party was given at HM's expense for the entertainment of local VIPs.

The selection of guests for this occasion required considerable tact, particularly among the 50 or so white residents. It was only too easy to make a *faux pas*. That first year we managed to make one by forgetting to arrange to collect the widow of a provincial commissioner who could not drive and had to be brought to the party.

June's first challenge was to produce refreshments for fifty or more official guests. She soon discovered that we had no fresh bread available for sandwiches and no dried yeast. Our cook made good bread, so June sent him off to get some yeast. He came back with a bottle of *pombe*

22. DO taking the salute at the King's Birthday Party, 1950.

(palm wine), swaying slightly and slurring his words as he reported on the excellence of his purchase.

June sent him away to sleep off his tasting session and set to work herself mixing and kneading enough dough

23. Inspecting police at King's Birthday Party, Malindi.

for six large loaves. From my office window I caught sight of him swaying down the beach with a pair of shorts over his left arm, which he was savagely attacking with a kitchen knife in his right hand. I sent a tribal policeman after him to find out what he thought he was doing. A cheerful Mkamba, he looked at me inanely and said, 'Thash a Kenya policeman in those trousers and he'ssh been interfering with my wife!'

Meanwhile, June and the grocer, Abbas Mohamedbhai, were searching the latter's storeroom for something to put in the sandwiches. She found three large, albeit ancient, tins of wild strawberries of unknown origin and, since no one in those days bothered about use-by dates, she took all three. In Turkana she had learnt how to make ice cream from condensed milk and she now set to work. Fresh dairy produce is of course an almost unobtainable luxury in areas infested with tsetse fly. The only problem remaining was to keep our new refrigerator, which worked with a kerosene lamp because there was no electricity, cold enough to freeze the ice cream. The north monsoon was blowing full blast and kerosene lamps do not like wind, but if one shut out the wind the room would become too hot for the freezer shelf to work. Somehow these problems were overcome and our strawberry ice cream was a great success.

VIPs from outside the district, who paid Malindi more than its fair share of attention, particularly in the school holidays and the game fishing season, were always time consuming. During our year in Malindi our list of visitors read almost like a government senior staff register. Starting with the acting governor, it continued with the postmaster general, director of establishments, director of public works, director of medical services, member for health and local government, and a senior official from the Colonial Office. More justifiably, we had visits from the provincial commissioner, the Bishop of Mombasa, the rural dean, the town planning adviser, and the provincial engineer, the latter coming in person at a weekend to relight the lighthouse lamp, which, for some unknown reason, had gone out.

The rural dean became a good friend and stayed with us on his visits. As a bachelor living alone in a hot climate, he had become accustomed to walking around his house in a state of relative undress. One day, however, while talking to June, he suddenly realized to his embarrassment that he had forgotten to put on his trousers. This did not prevent his subsequent preferment and he later became a bishop. At Easter he visited to take services at a small mission station inland at Jilore, which was in the charge of an African pastor, but when he arrived at the station he found the pastor in his garden digging vegetables and unprepared for any service. He had apparently mislaid his calendar and lost count of the date.

Not all visits were routine or official. An unusual and enjoyable visitor was Hugh Tracey, then secretary of the African Musical Society in South Africa and touring Africa with a recording team and van to record traditional African songs and music before they succumbed to Western influences. He had a warm personality and effective technique for getting things started, so wherever his van halted it was not long before an enthusiastic *ngoma* was in full swing, generally with much drumming. Prior warning of his arrival helped and on one such occasion I spent a particularly nostalgic night with him in the Arab village of Mambrui recording Swahili and Arab songs and dances. The men started the evening, but the women, not to be outdone and notwithstanding their veils, allowed him to make a very full recording of their songs and dances. For the men the sword dances were the most striking and memorable. Another impressive visitor was the Revd Lyndon Harries of the School of Oriental and African Studies, who was in search of old Swahili manuscripts and records. In a different category of visitor were the crew of

HMS *Mauritius*, and we found ourselves host to a couple of petty officers, of whom the district annual report records: 'Their visit was much enjoyed.' Fortunately, there was sufficient hotel accommodation to put up most of these visitors, but except in the very hot season both our spare room and guesthouse were always occupied.

As magistrate, I was naturally responsible for the maintenance of law and order, though Malindi was generally a law-abiding district. My duties could, however, sometimes be rather bizarre. On one occasion the normal somnolence of my courtroom was brightened by the Arab police inspector marching in two rather scantily dressed German women tourists in bikinis on a charge of creating a disturbance. As the evidence unravelled it became apparent that the disturbance was primarily in the mind of the inspector, but I was the custodian of public decency and the inspector's *heshima* was at stake. I fined the two women 5/– each, suggested they kept the receipts as souvenirs of their holiday, and told them to go back to their hotel and get dressed.

Ivory poaching was more serious and sometimes called for heavier sentences than I, as a third-class magistrate, could impose. Several of the tribal police had been professional ivory poachers before joining the police, and knew many of the routes and hiding places the poachers favoured. They were thus effective at finding poached and stolen ivory. Shortly after my arrival in Malindi the tribal police recovered an unusually large hoard (more than a ton) of poached ivory and I had a particularly villainous looking and unusually important collection of prisoners in custody. The facts were clear and, after hearing the evidence for the prosecution, I decided that this case was too important for me to hear, as in the event of a conviction I could not give a sentence of more than six months. I therefore stopped the hearing and referred the case to the Supreme Court in Mombasa. I was unlucky. The defendants were not short of money and engaged one of Kenya's leading counsel, an eloquent Irishman. The case was at the same time set down for hearing by a judge who was both new to the region and to the world of ivory poaching and smuggling. With great charm, counsel pleaded guilty on behalf of his clients and then, almost with tears in his eyes and without fluttering an eyelid, said in mitigation of sentence: 'M'lud, consider the enormous financial loss these poor men have suffered from having their ivory confiscated.' The judge gave them only three months each. I could – and would – have given them twice as much.

A more delicate case involved a European woman who came into my office one Saturday morning just before lunch saying that her husband, who was drunk, had threatened her with violence and turned her out of the matrimonial home. She wanted to go back into the house to collect her belongings before going to live with her mother. Could I please send a police constable to protect her? My legal training offered no guidance for this kind of request, but I did recall being warned against becoming involved in matrimonial disputes. I therefore phoned the assistant commissioner of police in Mombasa, who was about to leave his office for his Saturday pre-lunch drink at the Mombasa Club, for guidance about this proposed use of his police force. The request caught him unprepared and he asked for time to consult his manuals. I sent the distressed lady upstairs to be comforted by June. Ten minutes later he phoned back advising that I should send a constable with instructions to follow her back, but to remain on the other side of the road, and not to enter the house unless her husband assaulted her and she screamed for help. This seemed a reasonable compromise and I proceeded accordingly. Fortunately for all concerned her husband had passed out in a drunken stupor and she was able to pack and remove her bags without any need for police interference.

Sunday afternoons, when I usually hoped to enjoy a well-earned siesta, seemed to generate special problems. One Sunday I had to arrange for the relief of a passenger bus that had become bogged down in the mud. On another I had just started my siesta when there was a knock on the door. My driver Dixon, a Seventh Day Adventist who insisted on working on Sundays to assert his religious beliefs, appeared and said: 'Sir, man just come say there's baboon on woman's bed. He wants you go shoot him.' This seemed to me rather a fringe activity for the DO, but I picked up a rifle and followed him to a Swahili house in the township. Fortunately, by the time I arrived the baboon had tactfully departed down the beach leaving a somewhat distraught veiled lady on her bed.

Lunch invitations could generate another kind of problem, particularly when I forgot whom I had invited and when. The strategic layout of our house, however, was such that no one could approach without our seeing them well in advance. If caught unawares there was still time to recover our poise, get drinks out before the visitors arrived upstairs, and be waiting to greet them at the top of the stairs. We were just finishing our lunch one day when we saw two visitors arriving and I realized that I had forgotten to mention the invitation to June. Our cook, who had just brought in the coffee, rose to the occasion in great style, seized the whole lunch table and moved it round the corner of the veranda to clear and relay it, while June and I stopped our guests at the top of the stairs with drinks. We then sat down to a second lunch of salad from the refrigerator.

While we were in Malindi my mother came to visit us, though her first two days must have been very confusing, even embarrassing. She was due to arrive on a Wednesday and we had planned to hold a dinner party for a visiting VIP on Tuesday night to have it out of the way. On Monday morning June woke up with a pain in her middle that was sharper and more painful than the emergency appendix she had suffered at Oxford; she was feverish and shivery. Because our doctor was 40 miles away, I sent my driver with her so that she did not have to drive our heavy pick-up herself. What we did not know about our doctor, who was a charming young man in his first job who often stayed with us, was that he had missed out on his obstetrics training to volunteer to work in refugee camps in Europe. We were both hoping June was pregnant, but there were no instant tests in those days. He examined her carefully, told her firmly that she was not pregnant, nor ever would be because she was not the maternal type, and that there was nothing wrong with her except for a touch of malaria, for which he duly handed out quinine.

The nurse on duty, who had been present during the examination, looked extremely unhappy and, as June left, the other nurse, who was having her day off, met June and told her she must go to Nairobi immediately, that day. Irrespective of her mother-in-law, official entertaining or any other distraction, she must get the afternoon train from Mombasa that very day. She provided her with money and even a warm cardigan – it was cold in Nairobi – and forbade her to return home. 'Your life is at risk, as well as your ability to have babies. No, you cannot go to Mombasa hospital because they will ring up this doctor, and he will be furious. You must go to Mr Preston.' For once June took unwelcome advice. She had a terrible journey because the pain got worse, the train was late in Nairobi, there were no taxis and it was nearly 10 o'clock before she walked into the doctor's waiting room, which was crowded with hugely expectant ladies. The receptionist was expecting her and half an hour later Mr Preston was driving her to the hospital; at 12.30 he operated on an ectopic pregnancy. He then phoned me and said I should come to Nairobi immediately. Meanwhile, I had read in the shipping news that Mother's ship was arriving a day early, on that very Tuesday. I phoned kind friends, who met her and saw her onto the Malindi bus. That night she took June's place at the dinner table with great aplomb, though I did have to remind her to take the ladies to powder their noses while I conformed with Kenya custom and took the men into the rose garden. I soon learnt that the walled garden was the best place; there was less wind there.

As it was Mother's first visit to Kenya we felt we should show her as much of the country as possible. We decided to begin with the charming old town of Lamu. Unfortunately, the short rains were heavier than usual and the road to Lamu crossed a particularly glutinous stretch of black cotton soil just north of the ferry over the Tana River. We sent a telegram announcing our impending arrival to Lamu's only hotel, Petley's, and set out. The black cotton soil proved impassable for our pick-up and we spent an uncomfortable night in a mosquito-ridden guesthouse by the river at Garsen before returning defeated to Malindi. The following week, as the rain had eased off, we decided to try again, using the local bus owned by Sheikh Othman bin Dahman, in the belief that local skills might get us through. Unfortunately, the bus broke down with an unrepairable fault only 25 miles from Malindi and we had to limp back in bottom gear. The following week, hoping that a third attempt might be lucky, we set out again in our own truck and made it. After crossing by the ferry to Lamu Island, the hotel proprietor, Percy Petley, a retired rubber planter, greeted us on the steps of his hotel with the words: 'I'm glad you made it at last. When you didn't arrive I put your dinner in the fridge. I'll warm it up for you now.'

Petley's Hotel was located in an old Arab house with plenty of local colour and charm. However, the large rooms and high ceilings meant that the bedrooms consisted of a series of cubicles separated by partitions only six feet high. This helped to keep the cubicles cool, but it also meant that any noise or conversations could be heard in the other cubicles. It had also led to the development of an original kind of intermediate bathing technology. When a guest wanted a hot shower, Percy would send a servant with a bucket of hot water up a ladder. The guest would then stand under a kerosene tin fixed to the ceiling of his or her cubicle in the bottom of which a series of holes had been drilled. The servant would then stand outside the cubicle on a ladder and pour the water over the wall into the kerosene tin, thus generating a hot shower over the waiting guest. My mother declined the offer of a shower after dinner and retired early to bed after the long and tiring journey. June did not like to think how the servant knew exactly when to pour the water.

'I hope she sleeps well', said Percy of my mother, 'I thought she had better have a comfortable mattress so I gave her the one off my own bed.' In the morning we asked her if she had slept well. 'Not too badly,' she replied, 'except for the mosquitoes, which bit me.' We did not like to tell her that there were no mosquitoes in that part of Lamu and that bed bugs had been responsible for her itchy bites.

A few months later we took her on a boat trip round Lake Victoria. It was a fascinating journey, a new country for us all, and in Mwanza June was fascinated to stumble upon the grave of her mother's first husband who had been killed in the First World War in the first year of their marriage. On returning to Kenya an officious customs officer demanded to see our passports and, to our consternation, accused me of bigamy, which he informed us was not allowed in Kenya. How else could a man be travelling with two Mrs Knowleses?

Safari work was relatively less important in Malindi than in most districts. There was, however, a certain amount to be done both north and south of the Galana River, which divided the subdistrict into two parts. To the north lay the village of Mambrui and the Ngomeni peninsula with its salt works, which has since become the site of the Italian San Marco rocket launching project. Inland lay a number of Giriama locations, as well as some Sanya hunters. To the south lay the settlement of Gede and the Blue Lagoon of Watamu. A newly appointed government archaeologist, James Kirkman, was digging the mysterious jungly ruins of the ancient city, which he subsequently dated to the eleventh century. It had been abandoned two centuries later. No one knows exactly when or why it was so thoroughly and tidily evacuated. One of my predecessors had with great presence of mind sited a safari camp on the seashore at Blue Lagoon, which made an ideal spot for spending a week to write the district annual report. My mother loved the weekends we spent there, and June spent whole days following the tide out and then coming in with it, watching the wonderful fish in the coral reef. Both coral and fish have almost disappeared now.

One of the most famous Giriama at the coast, the witch doctor (*mganga*) Kabwere, whose reputation extended as far as Tanga where he went from time to time, lived near Gede. He was not only a skilful medicine man, but also a shrewd businessman and large-scale capitalist, owning several buses and a considerable amount of property. When the arrival of jet travel started the tourist boom, he shrewdly put up a notice on the main road outside his house saying 'Kabwere s/o Wanje – African Witch Doctor. Tourists strictly not allowed.' This of course acted like a magnet to the tourists.

Some years later when visiting Malindi, we met the district surgeon, Dr Rosinger, with whom we dined at the Sindbad Hotel. Rosinger mentioned having recently treated a German woman tourist for malaria who had commented that his fees were considerably lower than those of the African witch doctor. Rosinger did not like to ask her why she had consulted the witch doctor, but he knew Kabwere well and the next time he saw him said, 'I hear you have been guilty of a breech of professional etiquette by treating one of my patients. I will forget about that if you tell me what the lady came to see you about.' Kabwere replied, 'She asked me for a love potion. I supply plenty to tourists.'

Kabwere belonged to one of the leading hereditary Giriama families and was a son of Wanje, a celebrated Kambi elder from the Kaya Fungo. A *kaya* was the traditional holy meeting place of the *morhos* (councils) of the coastal Nyika peoples, such as the Giriama and the Kauma. By the time I arrived in Malindi the councils had ceased to have any political importance and served mainly as an excuse for a number of aged gentlemen to meet and drink beer.

Former chiefs and elders were usually buried in *kayas*. We visited Kaya Kauma near Garashi and met the elders there. However, little remained of the traditional *kaya*, for one of my predecessors, Champion (alias Bwana Chembe), had burnt it down in about 1913. There was, however, still visible a semi-circle of specially planted trees, in the centre of which were the sacred stone and sacred tree planted when the *kaya* was established. The elders told me that during its history the *kaya* had served as a stronghold and rallying place for the tribe, and had withstood two attacks, one by a Galla raiding party, which was repelled with the assistance of ten riflemen sent by the Arab headman in Mambrui, and the second by a gang of brigands whom the Kauma had themselves driven off. The *kaya* was also the meeting place of the elders, a kind of parliament, and every eight years or so power was handed down from one set of elders to the next.

Women were not usually allowed in, but they made an exception of June when she explained how annoyed her father had been when Bwana Chembe burnt the place down. Even then she had to take a special oath of secrecy. One elder admitted that yes, they did still bury someone alive at the handing over ceremony, usually a child, a very sick child. Yes, of course a girl child, no one would sacrifice a boy, would they?

With regard to development, the main aims of my work were to improve the health and social services, and to stimulate the agricultural economy and fishing industry by supporting the agricultural and fisheries officers. We took two important steps towards improving the health services while I was in Malindi – installing a piped water supply and building a new hospital staffed by a fully qualified medical officer. Early in my term of office I managed to persuade a wealthy Indian sugar farmer, Ghulamali Pirbhai, to donate a highly desirable plot near Vasco da Gama Point as the site for a new hospital. On the strength of this offer the director of medical services, Dr Farnworth Anderson, was persuaded to pay a visit and to agree both the proposed site and the allocation of the necessary building funds. He also promised to try and recruit a fully qualified district surgeon on a permanent basis. We had previously had a series of semi-qualified assistant surgeons – there were four in my year alone – before Dr Zeltan Rosinger was persuaded to come and make Malindi his home. Dr Rosinger's presence completely transformed the standard of medical care in

Malindi. Several years later he was instrumental in saving the life of our niece Caroline after she had been stung by a stonefish, through his prompt attention and thoughtful stocking of the necessary Australian serum.

There was, however, one disease that even he could not tackle. On a much later visit, June asked him about the incidence of VD at the coast – '100 per cent!' June put on her best academic expression: 'Look, I have read statistics and we both know that there is no such thing as 100 per cent!' The doctor replied sharply: 'I have been here for 20 years and I have never yet seen an Arab male who has not got, or recently had, VD! There is nothing I can do about it because they refuse to allow their women to come to me. A man may not examine them, even if the husband is present, so there is no point treating them.'

I was less successful at improving the township's sanitary services, even though we had two visits from a health inspector called Bernard Shaw. When I arrived, township cleansing arrangements depended on a number of refuse carts pulled by detainees from the detention camp. I did not approve of this use of detainees, and in any case we had a good year for tax payments and there were very few non-payers who usually provided the bulk of the detainees. I therefore decided to use some intermediate technology and purchased several donkey carts designed to carry refuse. At the same time I purchased four donkeys from our Somali butcher. Unfortunately, I failed to specify that they should be castrated and found we had bought four vigorous and highly-sexed jack donkeys. When tethered into the carts they started to fight each other. Two sewage carts going head on into battle is not a pleasant spectator sport, and the carts suffered considerable damage before they could be separated. I telephoned the veterinary surgeon in Mombasa to come and castrate the donkeys. They were found alas to be too old for this treatment and we had to revert to handcarts. The greatest improvement to health undoubtedly came from the provision of clean piped water to every household, even in the dry season. Families are large in Africa and June reckoned that it freed one person of every family for work elsewhere.

Fishery development policy was two pronged: the first objective was to acquire more knowledge of what lay off the coast and to expand inshore fisheries with the aid of powered boats; the second was to develop fish farming in the inland saltwater pools in the mangrove swamp areas. Our leading exponent of fish farming was 'Bonzo' Compton who had started to develop a fish farm near the salt pans at Ngomeni. Unfortunately, the process proved too capital intensive for his resources. He suffered considerable losses from predatory sea birds and when the fish somehow managed to start jumping over his barriers at high tide, he abandoned his courageous efforts.

According to the district records, attempts to develop the district's agricultural economy had defeated successive generations of administrators ever since the abolition of slavery disrupted the agricultural system at the beginning of the century. Most of the Arab plantations had never recovered from the loss of their labour force, and an attempt to introduce European-owned rubber plantations into the Sabaki Valley failed when the price of rubber slumped in the 1930s. By the time I arrived, efforts were being directed first towards an African settlement scheme at Gede growing subsistence crops as well as cash crops such as cotton, cashew nuts and kapok; second towards assisting the hinterland Giriama grow cotton and cashew nuts; and third towards planting sugar, mainly on Mr Pirbhai's plantation. It was an uphill fight, not only because the heat discouraged physical effort, but also because the uncertain rainfall and many agricultural pests made results somewhat speculative.

The various crop marketing policies, all of which seemed unsound, did not help the development of cotton, cashew nuts, maize and legumes. The cotton had to be sold at a fixed price to the local Indian ginnery, which, given half a chance, would under weigh the deliveries. I also caught it short-changing its hourly paid labour by altering the ginnery clock one hour back in the course of a day.

Cashew nuts were subject to a legal purchasing monopoly held by Lillywhite of Kilifi, which maintained an army of women and children to crack the nuts with hammers. The controlled buying prices appeared well below world prices and were too low to provide an incentive to harvest the nuts from the trees. A grower could make more money selling to the illegal free market. Maize and legumes were subject to another buying monopoly held by the Maize Control, a statutory corporation that bought at fixed prices, again low by free market standards. I distinguished myself by unwittingly authorizing a shipment of 'free market' maize and beans by coaster to Zanzibar.

My experience of Kenya marketing systems interested me enough to make a formal study of them and, five years later, I was able to finish a thesis entitled 'The Development of Agricultural Marketing in Kenya', which now lies in the vaults of the Bodleian Library. Unless Idi Amin destroyed it, there should also be a second copy in the Makerere College Library in Uganda. Two offshoots of my study of marketing were that while working in the treasury in the 1960s I became chairman of the Maize Price Advisory Committee, and in 1967 Kenyatta appointed me secretary of the Maize Commission of Inquiry, which held public hearings of evidence that provided the press with a three-week wonder.

A visit to the Coast Agricultural Show at Kilifi provided a fitting epilogue to our time in Malindi. I was a little surprised to be greeted by so many Africans with the friendly '*Jambo Bwana, Habari Zako?*' It was only when I got back to my car that it dawned on me that they were all detainees from our detention camp in Malindi who had taken the day off to visit the show; an arrangement had been made with a friendly lorry driver to take them over, but they were all back in camp the next morning for the roll call.

When I left Malindi I took the car, our luggage and one servant, leaving June only her newly acquired Alsatian, Poppet, to bring with her. She stayed on in Malindi for a week to finish a survey for the fishery officer on the household budgets of a group of fishing families. It was part of a health drive to see if the average earnings of fishermen were providing an adequate diet. June moved into the garden guesthouse my mother had recently occupied and, though she knew she had malaria, she went on working to finish the survey quickly. She did not, however, know she had cerebral malaria and was surprised one evening to find herself lying on the floor beside her supper table with Poppet licking her face and the cook, unsure what to do next, watching her have a malarial rigor. The following day she got herself to the Mombasa bus along with the camping luggage she had with her. I too had had an attack of malaria in Kiambu but managed to meet the train at Nairobi the following morning. That night was the third malarial day for us both and we both had high temperatures. At least there were two doctors in the Kiambu *boma* on whom we could call in the morning.

We must have slept heavily. Poppet barked and barked and only shut up when June snuggled her into bed. The next morning we discovered that robbers had been in our bedroom and stolen much of my wardrobe, including for some reason all my left-foot shoes, leaving me only the right-foot ones. The police were quick off the mark, found the rogues and returned some of the household linen. Until then, day or night, we had never locked a door and never had anything stolen. Indeed, empty jam jars and cast out saucepans had been returned to us in Turkana, so it was a daunting welcome to a new station, a reminder that at 15 miles outside Nairobi we were back in civilization.

7

Kiambu to Oxford Again

KIAMBU WAS very different from both Malindi and Turkana. The district was made up of a mixture of European-owned coffee farms and a Kikuyu reserve. There was a fringe of forest along the high western edge of the Aberdare mountains and sisal plantations along the low eastern border near the Athi plains. The district more or less encircled Nairobi and included the growing Dagoretti Corner market, so we had a generous share of peri-urban problems. The district's economy depended mainly on coffee, in European and Kikuyu areas, with pyrethrum on the high ground and sisal around Ruiru at the bottom. Pineapples and macadamia nuts were beginning to be planted in the coffee areas, and a little tea on the higher ground. A programme to plan and expand African markets absorbed a lot of our time. It was very green, and in the month of June somewhat chilly after two years in some of the hottest places.

Our main preoccupation was law and order. Kenya was in the run-up to Mau Mau and every week security reports were predicting further trouble and suspected oath taking. Police sorties based on informers' reports usually drew a blank, and a cat and mouse game was being played. The situation had its funny side and offered con men opportunities for commercial exploitation. In response to one informer's report a police party was sent to watch a certain forest clearing where suspicious activities appeared to be going on. An old man was bending over a wood fire, on which a pan appeared to be boiling. A succession of people came into the clearing, paid him some money and removed their trousers. They then bent over and he did something to their buttocks. After watching these activities with growing suspicion, the police pounced and arrested the old man. They found in the cooking pot a sterilized safety pin with which he had been pricking their bottoms, for which service he was charging them five shillings each. His clients thought they were being injected with some special medicine. At the time, penicillin had become widely available and was very popular. Among the Masai it was called '*Sindano ya kuzaa*', the injection of birth.

Kiambu gave us our first introduction to a *boma* society, with a *boma* club, golf course, collection of PWD-type IV houses, morning coffee parties and a social round of dinner parties at which gossip was exchanged and individual reputations scrutinized. The proximity of coffee farmers and of Nairobi, however, tempered *boma* life, so it was not a very inward-looking circle. When we arrived the DC was Miles North, a charming bachelor with an international reputation as a recorder of birdsong. This lent the *boma* an unusual special interest. We had not been in our house 24 hours before Miles appeared with his recording equipment. He had spotted a warbler in one of our trees and was anxious to record it. Unfortunately, at a critical point in the recording our cook's wife came from behind the house chasing a clutch of chickens, so a number of unwarbler-like clucks interrupted the bird-song, which did not improve the recording.

There were several district officers as well as a community development officer, so there was some scope for specialization. As I had some legal training and a degree in economics, I concentrated mainly on African court work and the planning and administration of district markets. The court work included a generous amount of land appeals from the judgments of African court elders. With the population expanding fast and land in short supply, an investment in land litigation could be very rewarding. It could equally prove a financial disaster for the litigant. Provided one was prepared to walk up and down hills and give sufficient time to each case, the work was very satisfying, though the number of cases that had to be heard each day and the number of *shamba*s (small farms) that had to be visited made it very tiring. It was generally unwise to dismiss an appeal without visiting the site. While African court records were in theory maintained in either English or Swahili, the literary abilities of court clerks and elders were limited and could give a misleading impression. A visit to a site often disclosed quite a different situation from that gleaned from reading the court report.

After giving a judgment of Solomon in a case involving ex-senior chief Koinanage, I found my reputation considerably enhanced among the Kiambu Kikuyu. Since one of my colleagues was known to deal with appeals in a peremptory manner, more than a fair share of land appeals began to come my way. At a time when Mau Mau's influence was growing and Kikuyu leaders had many Europeans under observation, the reputation I acquired for being fair, honest and impartial, I believe in retrospect, was of some importance in post-independence Kenya. It may even have been one of the factors that influenced President Kenyatta's decision to appoint me as secretary to the Kenya Maize Commission of Inquiry in 1967.

My work on African markets brought me into frequent contact with African businessmen. It was difficult work, with a number of 'no-win' situations. Dagoretti Corner, which was sandwiched between pressure from the Nairobi county council to restrict the market and from the Kikuyu to expand it without any of the necessary capital or communication facilities, was a good example. One of the main impediments to expanding African trade was the almost complete absence of postal and telephone facilities in the Kikuyu reserve. A trader might have to travel as many as 25 miles to post a letter or buy a stamp. There was also an almost complete absence of banking facilities, and even where facilities did exist, no way in which a trader could offer his premises or land as security for a bank loan. It was very difficult therefore for him to compete on equal terms with his Indian counterpart.

My land appeals also brought me into contact with the problems of African smallholder coffee growers. The Department of Agriculture, under pressure from European-owned coffee estates, which feared a spread of coffee plant diseases from the African areas to their plantations, was greatly restricting their activities. While there was obviously some justification for their fear, it was in my view exaggerated, and the draconian way in which the coffee controls were sometimes administered was a major factor in aggravating the political situation in the Kiambu district.

Roads in the reserve were for the most part appalling, though a drive had begun to improve them. Fortunately, the four-wheel-drive Land Rover had recently arrived in government service, and with a Land Rover one could generally count on arriving at one's destination, even in the rainy season. Road improvement was a high priority for the African district council, for its economic benefits were very rewarding to African transporters. A good example was the road to Githunguri on which a bus owner could hope to make one round trip daily before the road was improved, but afterwards, once the road had been tarred, could count on three or four trips daily.

Safaris absorbed quite a bit of my time in the reserve and could be very pleasurable. There was some good trout fishing, for the practice acquired during Mau Mau of dynamiting trout rivers with hand grenades had not yet begun. Also, from the western parts of the district, the views down onto the Rift Valley from 7500 feet above sea level were magnificent. Missions were thick on the ground, although the establishment of a new mission or church required the approval of the African district council. On one occasion when an application was being considered for a new church near Kiambaa, ex-chief Koinanage asked: 'Do they ring bells?' When told 'Yes,' he replied, 'Then I oppose it.'

A remarkable event occurred while we were in Kiambu. Jomo Kenyatta, who in those days was not well known and whose name June did not recognize although she had read his book *Facing Mount Kenya* ten years earlier, called to see her on three separate occasions. The drill was always the same. He came while I was away on safari. Four strapping young men in neat matching trousers and jerseys preceded him; two went to the back of the house where they stood looking into the living room, while the other two took up their position on the front veranda. Our cook would come and fetch June and only then would Jomo get out of his car and walk up to our front door. He started by saying he enjoyed the articles she was writing for the Swahili press; she responded politely and offered him tea. Our cook looked on disapprovingly; he was not a Kikuyu and did not like having to serve what he called 'one of those bad men'. They then had a stilted conversation. On the first occasion it went on for more than an hour and our little dog Poppet missed her evening walk. He offered June a teaching job at Githunguri Teachers' Training College. She was not sure where this was and said she would consult me. He would not tell her where to contact him; instead, he would call again. That weekend we drove to the college. It was an unimpressive, open sided concrete building under a thatched roof. The only reading matter was school science textbooks dating back to the beginning of the century, together with five-year-old copies of an English communist newspaper A glance through some exercise books showed that students had copied verbatim from both of these documents. There was no blackboard and no teaching facilities. And it was a difficult road; even our big Ford pick-up became straddled in the ruts.

The following week Jomo accepted June's refusal graciously. He drank his tea and ate his cake while our cook stood behind him making faces at June, who was sitting opposite him. He left with the smooth ease of an English gentleman. When I next went on safari he came again. This time he made a different offer – another school even further away, and June could teach economics and not English. She explained that she would have difficulty with transport, since we only had one car and when I went on safari I usually needed it. She added that we would be going on long leave in a few months' time, so she would be unable to complete a school year, which in Kenya ran from January to December. In all these visits he never once mentioned that her father had been his adviser and interpreter when he, as a young man, had appeared as a witness before the Hilton Young Commission in 1926, and had helped him prepare his case, which he later took to the British parliament. She only learnt this fact 30 years later when researching in Kew for her biography of her father *Oscar from Africa*.

After a few months in Kiambu I was surprised to receive a posting to the central secretariat. It was particularly surprising as I was due for home leave, and it hardly seemed worthwhile to involve us in yet another change of residence. Although only in the third year of our marriage we had already had four changes of house, and this was our fifth in one tour of duty. Although I was gaining useful experience, it did not seem to me that such frequent moves were conducive to either sound administration or continuity. And this time it was not even a house that was offered to us, but accommodation in a hostel on the Thika Road.

Fortunately, some of June's cousins had just bought a small farm with a wooden farmhouse in Chapore Lane, Limuru, opposite Gordhandas's sawmill. There was a dairy herd of 40 cows and they needed a tenant to supervise milking and deliver the milk to Wispers Farm every day, and collect the empties on the way home. June at once obtained a job in the East African Statistics Department, then situated in Bazaar Road. Although it was a 45-minute run to the office, it was very pleasant in the early morning to drive down Banana Hill with the dew on the ground and a panorama before us, which on a clear morning could stretch as far as Mount Kilimanjaro. The avocado trees that kept us supplied with a generous supply of large avocados were a pleasing feature of the farm. In the market they sold 20 for a shilling, and when we took a whole sack in, we received only 50 cents for the lot.

It was here that the Mau Mau first impinged on our lives, though we did not realize it at the time. Almost at once, the farm headman came to us and said he wanted to leave. At the same time our Mkamba cook told us that his brother, who had worked on a well-known dairy farm, was looking for a job. When another, and then another, man came to us wanting to leave, and in each case our cook found a replacement, we became suspicious. Our cook was devoted to June and she had a serious talk with him, pointing out that we would only be on the farm for a short time and that it was unfair to replace all the local Kikuyus with his friends and relations from his own tribe far away. He would not look at her, but kept repeating: 'Very bad here, very bad people.' A few months after we left the terrible massacre at Lari occurred, when many Africans were slaughtered, the women and children particularly brutally.

I was posted to the establishments division of the central secretariat. At that time, the whole secretariat was housed in a few wooden penthouses that had been built on top of the flat roof above the law courts. I worked in one of these offices, which were uncomfortably cold in the early morning and unbearably hot in the afternoon. The work was mostly dull, consisting largely of controlling travel allowances and mileage rates. I was also made secretary of the European civil service advisory board, a job that provided some human interest when the board met to interview candidates for vacant posts. I learnt some useful tips on how to be interviewed and to present oneself to a board. I was also the official side secretary of the Central Whitley Council, which had been set up to smooth out disagreements with the staff associations on terms of service. While I held this job I had to work out a new scale of mileage allowances for privately owned vehicles used on official duty. I believe that in a small way I was able to make a useful contribution to greater efficiency in administration by slanting the new rates so that four-wheel-drive Land Rover owning was given some encouragement.

After six months in the secretariat I had completed a three-year tour, and, having served 18 months of this in the Northern Frontier Province, I had seven months of leave due to me. About this time we had the good news that June, who had been under the attention of a Nairobi doctor, was pregnant and the baby was due the following March. With seven months leave due, the opportunity to take a sabbatical year at Oxford and to study agricultural marketing appeared too good to miss. June was also anxious to study anthropology. If the baby arrived as expected at Easter, she might even manage to complete an academic year and the diploma course.

It was easier to arrange for our degree courses than to find accommodation. June's former tutor at St Anne's, Peter Ady, agreed to act as my supervisor for a thesis on the development of agricultural marketing in Kenya, and

June had no difficulty getting accepted for the diploma course in anthropology. She was careful not to tell them about the baby before it became obvious, when she was already established on the course. In the event, she need not have worried. The professor of anthropology, who was the devoted father of seven children, was most sympathetic and his secretary sat knitting tiny garments.

We were able to find temporary accommodation at the Colonial Services Club in South Parks Road, which was maintained primarily for the benefit of colonial service recruits and officials undergoing training courses in Oxford. Meanwhile, we asked Walters & Company in Turl Street, which had a reputation for arranging anything the colonial service needed and had even supplied and shipped a piano for us to Kenya, to look around for accommodation.

They found us furnished rooms in a modern semi-detached house of interwar vintage in Cowley. These were hardly ideal, however, for only a folding partition separated us from our landlords and almost every word of conversation on one side could be heard on the other. When a guest came for tea one day and passed a remark to June about our 'obscene-looking teapot', we felt conscious of the embarrassed silence on the other side of the partition. Our bedroom accommodation was also cramped, and, being pregnant, June did not appreciate me keeping her awake at night when I had a hacking cough. As a result I had to pass a night in an armchair in our sitting room coughing hard.

The friend who had been so rude about our landlady's teapot told us that they were leaving their pleasant first-floor flat in Norham Gardens, so we moved there as soon as possible. It was within easy walking distance of the parks and of the Institute of Anthropology, then in a Victorian villa in Parks Road, ideal for June who had been forbidden a bicycle. When her Nairobi doctor heard we were coming to Oxford, he referred to his Edinburgh medical directories and found the name Chasseur-Moir – anyone who had trained at Edinburgh with him must be good! That he was the Nuffield Professor of Gynaecology meant little to him, and I doubted if such a high flyer would have time for my wife. However, the professor was a fellow of Oriel, my own college, and readily agreed to take her on.

We were very happy in our flat. My mother and sister joined us for Christmas and June had first-class care throughout her pregnancy. The Easter vacation started, but Christopher showed no sign of budging and the good professor went away for the Easter weekend. Meanwhile, I had ordered a new Land Rover and June decided to accompany me to Birmingham to drive the vehicle back. The early Land Rovers had very short wheelbases, which caused them to rock quite roughly, even on British roads, and the drive back did the trick. The young doctor working under Chasseur-Moir had broken his right arm two days earlier and had it in plaster and, when after 48 hours of labour he decided that forceps would be necessary, things became uncomfortable for all concerned. The doctor kept saying it was hurting him more than her. That night 14 babies were born instead of the usual two or three, possibly because if a baby were born before 6 a.m. on 5 April the father received a full income tax allowance for the child for the previous financial year. This did not apply to us because we paid Kenya income tax and our tax year started on 1 January. The rush of cases meant, however, that all the gas cylinders were empty and no one had time to get fresh ones.

Having ensured Christopher's safe arrival I went to Cambridge to attend a Colonial Office conference. I had not been there more than two days when I received a phone call from the doctor in Oxford asking me to return as soon as possible because June had a high fever. I came back at once to find that she had managed to convince the doctors she was suffering from malaria and not puerperal fever and was responding well to antimalarials, whereas she had not responded to the penicillin they had prescribed her. She had also given the Oxford medical students a rare opportunity to witness a genuine malarial rigor. One effect of the fever was that she had been moved from an amenity bed to an isolation ward to prevent the spread of puerperal fever. The practical significance of this change appeared to be that instead of being asked whether Mrs Knowles would like coffee, which was then served in a pot on a tray, in the isolation ward a mug of tea would be shoved in front of her with a cheerful: 'Here yer are, luv!'

Christopher was a fine boy, fair-haired, blue-eyed and weighing in at nine pounds. He was so full of fight that he was nicknamed Puncher Knowles, for he would wave his tiny fists at the nurses if his cries were not immediately answered. Back at the flat, under the loving care of his parents and grandmother, he flourished and by the beginning of the summer term he was ready to lie in his pram in the Institute of Anthropology garden where all the staff, including the professor, paid him lots of attention. June completed her diploma and obtained one of the best results of the year.

Meanwhile, I slogged away in the Rhodes House library brushing up on my Kenya history and attending lectures on agricultural economics theory and practice at the Agricultural Economics Research Institute, while Peter Ady kept an eye on my general progress. My research into the development of agricultural marketing almost turned into a study of the history of modern Kenya. Under Lord Delamere, then later the Member for Agriculture Cavendish-Bentinck, marketing policy had been geared towards protecting the settler farmer. I found the knowledge I acquired during the course of my thesis very helpful when I went to the treasury, particularly when I became the chairman of both the Maize Price Advisory Committee and the Duty Drawbacks Committee, and a member of the East African Tariffs Advisory Committee.

As the summer term of 1953 progressed at Oxford the Mau Mau movement in Kenya was gathering strength and I was half-prepared for an early recall. Fortunately, this did not happen until after the end of the academic year, so I was able to complete the residential requirements for my B.Litt. degree. I had planned to return by sea with the Land Rover, with June following by air. I now had to return by air, but June did not want to take a young baby through the Red Sea during the summer heat. There was no air-conditioning on ships in those days and she knew how hot it could get. The problem was that if the Land Rover stayed in England any longer it would become subject to full English taxes, and unless a member of the family travelled with it we would lose tax advantages at the Kenya end. June then suggested she take the baby and the Land Rover to Austria to stay with friends and attend an archaeological conference.

I decided to drive her to Austria and then go on to Rome, where many flights from London to Nairobi stopped to refuel. We had a wonderful trip down the Rhine Valley, our first visit to Germany since the war. We enjoyed both the food and wine, which were more plentiful than in England. The scenery was stunning and there were comparatively few tourists. I felt very alone as I waved goodbye to June, with Christopher bouncing up and down in her arms, at Brixlegg station on the train to Rome where I was to catch my plane.

I was posted to Kisii in South Nyanza. I wrote up my thesis over the following two years, mainly in early mornings before breakfast, so was able to take my viva (oral) examination when next on leave.

8

Kisii

I T WAS AUGUST 1953 when I flew back to Kenya, leaving June to return by sea from Genoa with our three-month-old baby and new Land Rover. She stayed a few more weeks in the Tyrol and then, accompanied by Doris Kindl, her Austrian cousin, left for Genoa. Sightseeing *en route* they left Chris asleep in his carrycot in the Land Rover while they went to look at Milan cathedral. On returning to the Land Rover they found it surrounded by a crowd of Italian women cooing at Chris who by this time had awakened.

June's voyage was uneventful apart from Chris managing to pick up head lice. I went to Mombasa to meet them and to help drive the Land Rover up to Kisii. It was the start of the short rains and not only was the Mombasa road muddy in places but rivers in full spate had also flooded several of the Irish bridges. With a four-wheel-drive Land Rover we were able to negotiate all these rivers in style. Unfortunately, we encountered a number of friends and acquaintances *en route* who were less lucky and we had to spend a considerable amount of time and petrol towing them either through the flooded

rivers or through patches of black cotton soil. After
pulling the last one, May Buxton, through the Makindu
drift we headed for Nairobi, only to run out of petrol at
about midnight on the Athi plains 15 miles short of
Nairobi. We were on the edge of Mau Mau country.
Fortunately, we had passed a farm about a quarter of a
mile back, so I took our spare can and set out to find it
while June, nursing a wheel brace for self-defence, locked
herself and Chris in the Land Rover. I was lucky. The
farm belonged to a white hunter who came to the door
brandishing a shotgun, but I got my petrol. We eventually arrived at the Norfolk Hotel at 3 a.m.

Kisii was the administrative headquarters of the South
Nyanza district, which had not then been divided into its
Gusii and Luo tribal components. It was therefore a very
large and important district, comprising at least three
tribal and racial groups, Bantu, Nilotic and Nilo-Hamitic,
with a large headquarters that employed 20 Europeans. It
was a prosperous district producing important cash crops
like coffee, pyrethrum and sugar, and a substantial township was developing to provide services like transport and
banking. Two banks opened branches while I was there,
and a former white hunter, Dick Gethin, ran a transport
service. There was also a small European owned hotel.

European social life revolved around the Kisii club
with its nine-hole golf course and tennis courts. It was a
boma par excellence with a tightly prescribed social peck-
ing order and a routine of dinner party invitations. As
bomas go it was a happy one, with a minimum of social

friction and carefully watched over by the DC Dennis Hall and his wife. We did not play golf and our tennis was poor, but June took part in amateur theatricals and we gave our quota of dinner parties. These occasionally brought unforeseen surprises, particularly since our Mkamba cook had a fondness for the bottle and our Turkana houseboy, Kionga (who had put the turkey eggs in the refrigerator in Lokitaung), was liable to do unexpected things. One house, which the district foreman occupied, contained a poltergeist, which occasionally enlivened dinner parties by throwing the china around. While dining one evening with Michael Downham, the resident magistrate, and his wife, our cook Muya burst into the dining room with his lip in shreds and bleeding profusely. He had apparently returned the worse for wear after a drinking session, called Kionga a 'mshenzi' (an uncivilized person) and been rewarded with a broken bottle across his face. On another evening when we had planned a dinner party, Muya was nowhere to be found. A Coca-Cola drinking Seventh Day Adventist missionary eventually returned him to us after having found him drunk in his garden, implying that if we employed a Catholic cook, what else could we expect?

The main Knowles contribution to livening up the *boma* was the introduction of 'Neddy Knowles', a donkey we bought to carry Christopher in June's old riding basket. We kept him in our garden, from where periodically he would let off ear-splitting brays that could be heard all around the *boma*. Every day after tea June would lead Neddy down to the club with Christopher on his back. He attended the club so regularly that after a while he was invited into the bar and made an honorary member, the only donkey in Kenya to enjoy such a distinction.

June considerably broadened the cultural life of Kisii. Having just completed her diploma in anthropology she was anxious to use her newly-acquired knowledge, so when she heard stories of a sub-tribe of metal smelters who had made spears for the Masai and were said to have smelted gold, she decided to investigate. There were several small European-owned gold mines in South Nyanza and it seemed quite possible that this story was true. Having been given a lead to a farm on the Sotik border, where pits these metal smelters had used in the past were reportedly to be found, one Saturday afternoon we drove to Sotik in the Land Rover and soon located the pits in question. To our delight June quickly found what appeared to be the remains of a crucible for smelting metal and we returned to Kisii with our valuable treasure. We carefully preserved it until our next leave when June took it to the Pitt Rivers Museum in Oxford. She handed it to the curator, Mr Pennyman, who seemed delighted and promised to get it identified and classified. On our following leave, when June returned to the Pitt Rivers expecting to receive a warm welcome, Mr Pennyman greeted her with a long face and said: 'We spent 18 months getting that artefact identified. It was a piece of an old German car battery from the First World War.'

Kisii was the site of a minor unreported battle in the

First World War. In 1914, neither the British nor the Germans in East Africa were prepared for war and the German governor of Tanganyika had even hoped that, by some means or other, perhaps under the terms of the Congo Basin Treaty, East Africa might be excluded from a general declaration of war in Europe. Unfortunately, this could not be arranged and he, Tanganyika's civilian governor, now faced a military commander, Colonel von Lettow-Vorbeck, who considered it his duty to tie up as large an allied army in East Africa as possible, thus weakening the forces against Germany in Europe. After some initial delay Lettow-Vorbeck initiated a number of probing actions against the Kenya–Uganda Railway, which was a particularly vulnerable target.

Both sides showed a considerable amount of amateur military enthusiasm and Boy Scout expertise was at a premium. The main German thrust was in the vicinity of Taveta and Voi, but in late 1914 a drive was launched from Musoma in the direction of Kisii. British intelligence was poor and credited the Germans with more strength than they in fact had, so the British evacuated the Kisii *boma* and the advancing Germans occupied it. The DC who owned a piano left a note in his house requesting them to refrain from pouring beer from his food store down his piano in the event of any drinking parties. The Germans, who appreciated his gesture of leaving them his beer supply, made his house their headquarters while they regrouped and rested before resuming their advance towards Kisumu.

When the German capture of Kisii was not immediately followed by a further advance, the British
company commander sent out scouts under a white
hunter called Ross, who reported that the Germans had
only about two companies and a couple of Maxim guns.
By this time British reinforcements had arrived across the
lake from Uganda, and, strengthened by half a company
of KAR with a Lewis gun and some Uganda police, the
British force commander decided to ambush the German
force as it left Kisii. He distributed his force on the hills
around the Kisii *boma*, covering the main road with his
Lewis gun. When the Germans resumed their advance,
goose-stepping down the road, the white officers and
NCOs were an easy target for the Lewis gun, and white
casualties were disproportionately heavy. The Germans
took cover by the side of the road and fired back until
early afternoon, by which time both sides were feeling the
heat and running out of ammunition, and the British
withdrew to regroup. After a night's rest they were ready
to advance on the *boma*, only to find that the Germans
had withdrawn during the night, leaving their wounded
NCOs to protect the DC's bungalow from looting by Kisii
tribesmen. The British quickly reoccupied Kisii, leaving
Ross's scouts to harass the retreating Germans. Ross, who
disliked Germans, is reported, according to a story Salim
Mkuu who served as one of his scouts recounted, to have
found a German missionary eating breakfast under a tree,
shot him and then eaten his breakfast.

As a senior district officer with some legal background,

I was put in charge of African courts; in a multi-tribal district that postwar development and new cultural contacts were changing rapidly. This was to prove a much more interesting assignment than I had expected. As in Kiambu, I had to settle numerous land appeals, so spent many days walking up and down the Kisii Highlands with court assessors, inspecting judgments on the ground and hearing appeals. On the whole it was surprising how equitable most of the judgments were. The most interesting work legally was reviewing cases involving family law with regard to inheritance, divorce and the custody of children. I was fortunate to arrive some time after it became obligatory on the lower courts to record the grounds of a judgment, and so there was already a valuable collection of judgments and of case law. In addition to the cases I had to review, I spent some time reading old judgments and obtained material for an article that was subsequently published in 1956 in the London *Journal of African Administration*.[1]

The legal rights of women were in a state of evolutionary change. A cause of action might be recorded as 'I want my mother-in-law' or 'my mother-in-law bewitched me', but such plaints were in fact becoming a way of expressing some very modern concepts. A mother-in-law's claim for divorce on the grounds of witchcraft

1. Oliver Knowles, 'Some Modern Adaptations of Customary Law in the Settlement of Matrimomial Disputes in the Luo, Kisii, and Kuria Tribes of South Nyanza', *Journal of African Administration* (London, January 1956).

would usually prove to be a case of what the Americans would have called mental or moral cruelty. A suit to obtain possession of a mother-in-law usually signified a property dispute following a death or divorce. An encouraging feature of the situation was the apparent willingness of elders, indeed their concern, to adapt their family law to changing social circumstances. While visiting Kisii on a farewell trip in 1969 just before we left Kenya, I was intrigued to find that my article was being quoted to substantiate a particular point of law. I hope future historians will credit British administrators and African elders for developing a remarkably fair legal system at very low cost.

Court work brought me into contact with many interesting facets of district life. In Gwassi location I heard about the snake of Gwassi and the splinter sect *Dini ya Mariamu* (Religion of Mary). On Rusinga Island I found out about the dissident faction that paddled across the lake and settled on Rusinga after a palace revolution against the *kabaka* of Buganda. I was told about radio activity on Homa Mountain and the hazards of pitching a tent on it. On the Masai border I met *Ole Mzungu* (son of the European), a court elder whose light skin colour suggested that his father must have been a peripatetic German.

A principal task of the provincial administration was to provide back-up support for the African district councils formed in response to a Colonial Office drive to develop responsible local government. The secretary of the South Nyanza Council at this time, the highly respected Paul Mboya, had an excellent relationship with the DC, Dennis Hall, and the council was increasing its revenue and expanding its activities. Sport and athletics had benefited from the expansion and there was a considerable amount of indigenous talent awaiting development. We were lucky in that the influential Senior Chief Musa, an ex-officio district councillor for a Kisii location, took a personal interest in sport and in promising young athletes. Musa was a great character and a natural leader who combined old traditions (he had 30 wives and countless children) with a modern outlook on many subjects, such as coffee growing and sport. Despite his 30 wives he employed a cook, for he found he could not rely on his wives to feed him. He was the first to recognize that at 6500 feet above sea level, the Kisii Highlands provided a natural training ground for long distance runners. School children had to run home from school or be caught in the daily late afternoon downpours.

Dennis Hall had recognized the potential of sport to put Kisii on the map. When I arrived the Kisii stadium had just been completed and I was put in charge of it and of sporting activities. My sporting administration days in Kisii were notable for one major success and for one miscalculation. My success was to spot the potential of Nyandika Mayoro, Kenya's first great long-distance runner, and to appoint him community development assistant in charge of the stadium. This was critical to his progress because it gave him a regular basic salary, time for training, and he was on the spot to take advantage of lessons from visiting coaches. He had previously been a veterinary scout and his running had had to take a second place. Once appointed as a CDA he trained for the Commonwealth Games in Melbourne and began a running career from which he never looked back. He has since been followed by other famous Kisii long-distance runners.

My miscalculation was to build two changing rooms at the stadium, one for the home team and one for the visiting team. While the home team always used its changing room, visiting teams would always change off the ground and then enter it by jumping over the barrier. I subsequently found out that they were attempting to circumvent any possible endeavour by the local witch doctor to cast an unlucky spell on the visitors' changing room and entrance gate – just as every leading English team has a mascot, so most Kenyan teams have a witch doctor.

When we arrived in Kisii, Mau Mau was at its peak and Kikuyu tribesmen who had settled there were being rounded up and sent back to their tribal lands. While awaiting transport, they were detained in camps with the women and children kept separate from the men. June and other wives would go down daily to check on them and ensure that the children were being properly fed and the women not molested. Fortunately, South Nyanza was almost completely free of Mau Mau and we could concen-

trate on development. With CD&W (colonial development and welfare) funding and help from the Colonial
Development Corporation, services were rapidly being
increased. In Kisii a major effort was put into developing
cash crops, as well as livestock, fisheries and social
services, particularly hospitals and dispensaries. We had
some setbacks, and I particularly recall the gloomy face of
a livestock officer on discovering that the pedigree
breeding bull he had issued to a farmer had been sold for
meat. But overall, it was a time of rapid development,
rising incomes and considerable optimism. We were
amused when a nursing sister in our new hospital
recounted finding the husband of a maternity patient in
bed with his wife in the hospital ward – and still wearing
his boots!

It was clear from my mother's letters that she was
feeling exceedingly ill, so I wrote to my uncle asking for
news and offering to apply for compassionate leave. He
wrote back saying that the doctor thought I should not
come because it would make her think that she was more
seriously ill than she was. However, his letter arrived only
after the telegram announcing her death. We had planned
to spend Christmas with friends near Nairobi and to visit
a game park afterwards, but now I wanted to go to
England for her funeral. June said she would come to
Nairobi with me and then go on to the game park with
our friends. I obtained a flight on Christmas day in a
South African Airways Constellation. My only cheerful
memory of that day was watching Christopher sitting in a

high chair eating an enormous breakfast in the Nakuru Hotel dining room. Being Christmas, the plane was almost empty and I was able to stretch out on three seats for the night. In the morning I had a wonderful view of snow on the mountains of Greece.

I returned in early January and, on my birthday a month later, while reviewing a case of cattle theft at Subakuria courthouse on the Masai border, a steel-helmeted Kenya policeman rode up on a bicycle with a telegram to say that our second son Nick had been born. June had had a false alarm a month earlier and when our *boma* doctor made it clear that he felt uneasy about delivering the baby, June had gone to Nairobi to await events. I sent her a long telegram of congratulations. Only years later when clearing out a drawer did she find my copy of the original telegram and realize that the post office clerk had only sent her 'well done' and pocketed the cash for the remaining words.

We left Kisii in July 1955 with a feeling of accomplishment. We had enjoyed our time there, but were glad not to have to spend the rest of my colonial service career in *boma*s.

9

Treasuries:
Nairobi and London

ON COMPLETING our tour in Kisii in 1955 we went on leave. A large part of the leave was spent clearing up my mother's house in Warrington, and as this was my childhood home it was an emotional experience. While on leave I submitted my thesis entitled 'The Development of Agricultural Marketing in Kenya'; I was duly examined in Oxford and awarded a B.Litt. degree. A by-product of my thesis was that I received an invitation to participate in a private conference being held at Nuffield College in October 1955 to discuss (and later submit a confidential statement to the government on) the Royal Commission's report on East Africa. There were 40 participants, including most of the big names in African affairs like Arthur Creech-Jones, P. T. Bauer, S. H. Frankel, F. S. Joelson, Harry Oppenheimer, Oliver Woods, Margery Perham and William Gorell Barnes. I felt highly honoured to have been asked to participate, particularly when I was invited to intervene in the discussion.

On my return to Kenya I was posted to the Treasury. This was then a stimulating place in which to work because it was enjoying a vintage period intellectually. The post-Mau Mau reconstruction of the economy was just beginning, and the consolidation of the debt incurred in fighting Mau Mau was a problem we needed to address. The Swynnerton Plan, named after the director of agriculture Roger Swynnerton, had just proposed an imaginative approach to African agricultural development. Because 65 per cent of the development budget had been allocated to agriculture, the treasury, which combined the portfolios of finance and development planning, was heavily involved in both planning and funding the scheme. Frequent financial discussions with the Colonial Office were needed.

Fortunately, there was an extremely able team at the treasury, of a calibre possibly unique in colonial history. The member for finance and development planning, Ernest Vasey, a former actor and cinema manager, had graduated to the treasury through serving both in local government and as mayor of Nairobi. With his innovative, rather theatrical personality and Churchillian taste for cigars, he brought to finance an imaginative yet realistic approach, which was seen at its best on budget day. Kenneth Mackenzie, the treasury secretary, provided a solid base for other people's ideas and, having worked in the UK treasury as a 'beachcomber' (a colonial service officer on secondment), had useful inside knowledge of the Colonial Office and UK government, which he deployed in financial negotiations. John Butter, the deputy secretary, was an ex-ICS officer whom, as I mentioned earlier, I first met in Manipur state during the war paying out cash to the army because all the local treasury clerks had run away following the bombing of Imphal. He was not an economist, but he took a keen interest in money markets and financial services. He later became permanent secretary to the treasury and, on Kenya's independence, moved to Abu Dhabi, where he was a very successful financial secretary and possibly one of the most highly paid civil servants in the world. The most outstanding of the younger officers was Philip Haddon-Cave, an Australian from Tasmania who had come to the treasury via the East African statistical department and who, along with Vasey, was responsible for starting the Economics Club of Kenya. He brought a new approach to development planning. Philip later transferred on promotion to Hong Kong, where he rose to become financial secretary and then chief secretary. Other officers of above average ability included Geoffrey Ellerton, Frank Gilboy, Elizabeth Usher, Joan Tyrrell, John Riley and M. Y. Khan.

I was lucky with my first assignment, which was to relieve Haddon-Cave at the development planning desk while he was on leave. This desk included the job of joint assistant secretary to the Council of Ministers' development committee. Frank Corfield, an ex-Sudan service officer who was in the Cabinet Office, was the other joint secretary. The desk also included the job of treasury representative on the board of trustees of the Coryndon Museum, a function that frequently brought me into contact with the distinguished naturalist and archaeologist, L. S. B. Leakey. I also became secretary of the Economics Club of Kenya and a member of the finance committee of the United Kenya Club, both of which brought me into regular contact with Ernest Vasey.

On arrival in Nairobi we had to live in one room in a crowded hotel on the Ngong Road before being allotted a house on Bernhard Estate. This was a new housing estate near Dagoretti Corner, for which the treasury had negotiated a complex contractor–finance purchase arrangement with a wealthy local financier called Israel Massada. The houses were unimaginatively designed, but they were an improvement on our earlier government houses. The garden was unmade and consisted of heavy black cotton soil, which turned into thick mud when it rained. Our small boys loved the mud.

Bernhard Estate had originally been a coffee plantation belonging to St Austin's Mission, the coffee-growing pioneers who imported the Jamaican Blue Mountain variety of arabica coffee bean into Kenya. The estate was on the edge of the Kikuyu Reserve, which in turn bordered on the Nairobi National Park, so an occasional jackal or leopard would visit us at night. The area was home to the Limuru Hunt, which kept its hounds at the residence of Derek Erskine, a colourful character who lived in Riverside Drive. He was an ex-Etonian who ran a wholesale grocery business in Nairobi. Periodically both huntsmen and hounds would sweep through Bernhard Estate in search of jackals. On one occasion a concealed leopard caused a stampede of the hounds.

We remained in Bernhard Estate for one year. It was here that Christopher was diagnosed with Perthes' disease, and we were told he would have to be in hospital for two years. The matron of Gertrude's Garden Children's Hospital was away and it was not running smoothly in her absence. After a couple of weeks in hospital Christopher was so unhappy and going downhill so fast that June decided she must nurse him at home, though it would mean giving up the teaching on which she had just embarked at the technical college. The doctors opposed her decision on the grounds that the nursing was too specialized, so she advertised for an orthopaedic nurse. She had an immediate response from someone who had been matron of the specialist Perthes' ward at the hospital in Carshalton, with 40 young boys in her charge. She was recovering from a personal crisis and wanted a quiet job. She came daily to wash and massage Christopher, who was still in traction, but he soon looked much better and regained his interest in life.

In 1957, with a small legacy from my Aunt Bertha, we bought our own house in the Spring Valley area, for it seemed that I would be remaining in the central government. The house was much nearer the centre of Nairobi, gave us more space, and had both a tennis court and a small cement swimming pool. Mark was born soon after we moved and no sooner had we brought him home than

I was offered a two-year secondment to the UK treasury in Whitehall. Such opportunities did not occur often and, since it suggested I had been identified for promotion as a 'high flier', I did not feel I could turn it down. Mark was born at the end of May and in November we let our new house for two years and moved to London with our three small boys.

Finding accommodation raised an immediate problem. There were no special arrangements to help 'beach-combers' (the treasury name for officers on secondment from the colonial service) and only with very careful management was my salary sufficient to support a family of three sons. We started off in a hotel in Kensington that offered special facilities for young children. From there, with the help of estate agents, we eventually located a maisonette that was within our means above the Society Wedding Press in Marloes Road. The maisonette was rather run down, but our landlords, who owned the Society Wedding Press and who made their living by following up engagement notices in the *Daily Telegraph* and *The Times*, were easy-going people and we had the use of a small garden, which was invaluable for putting out a small rubber paddling pool on a hot summer's day. We used to watch our landlords with fascination as they set out on a Saturday morning to photograph 'without obligation' their latest victims.

My first impressions of the UK treasury were deeply depressing. After the sunshine, new office building and innovative optimism of the Kenya treasury, Great George

Street, with its lavatory brick walls, obsolete heating system, inefficient secretarial and typing-pool facilities, and a canteen reminiscent of the worst type of 'British restaurant', were enough to chill the spirits of any beachcomber. I was posted as a principal to the trade and industry division under the kindly Alec Grant and thrown in head first, on the assumption that I knew both the subject matter and how the system worked. I was responsible to Grant for all Board of Trade, DSIR (Department of Scientific and Industrial Research) and Royal Society expenditure. The higher executive officer deputed to support me must have found me quite a liability. I soon managed to develop a comfortable working relationship with my main contact at the Board of Trade, Pat Hypher, with whom I played squash at lunchtime in the squash courts at the Duke of York Steps. The scientific component of my work gave me an entrée to a number of scientific open days and Royal Society symposia.

Towards the end of my first year duties were reorganized. The trade and industry division was broken up and a new 'arts and science' division formed, to which I was transferred, along with the scientific votes of expenditure. There was no clear logic behind the creation of this division, and my portfolio was an extreme example of the British cult of the amateur, for I was expected to make recommendations on a very diverse range of subjects. These included Professor Lovell's radio telescope, food and shoe research, the National Physics Laboratory, the repair of Roman villas and ancient monuments, and making decisions on whether or not to accept historic houses and estates in lieu of death duty. It was highly educational for me, though probably less satisfactory for my clients. None of the subjects bore any relevance to the work I had done in Kenya, and I had very little knowledge of any of them. But then nor I suspect did some of my superiors.

Decision making could be a lengthy process. A case file on a complex matter that started at assistant principal level, could spend several weeks acquiring progressively more erudite and often contradictory minutes as it progressed up the chain through principal, assistant secretary, under secretary, third secretary, second secretary and, on an important file, to first secretary, thence to our political masters. Drafting replies to parliamentary questions and speculating on possible supplementary questions provided an amusing pastime. In complex matters a working party could be appointed and I had the good fortune to be appointed secretary to one under Burke Trend, then a third secretary, to advise on the proposals for a national science reference library. This was not a new proposal. It had been on the books since the turn of the century and a series of working parties had tackled the subject. I was determined that our working party should be the one to end all further working parties on this subject, but it was a good many years and several other working parties later before a decision was taken to go ahead and establish the library. Burke Trend had a very clear brain and a masterly grasp of English and it was a pleasure to work under him, so it was no surprise to me when he was later appointed secretary to the Cabinet Office.

I managed to survive my two years without making too many serious mistakes, though one could have led to a minor parliamentary embarrassment had the financial secretary, Sir Edward Boyle, not skilfully taken it in hand. The problem arose through my misunderstanding of some legal advice from the treasury solicitor, and I found I had undertaken to sell the same cottage in the Lake District, which had been taken in lieu of death duties, to two different would-be purchasers, both of whom were influential Cambridge dons.

The case of the Jodrell Bank telescope was a fascinating one, both for its scientific importance and as an illustration of how the British system worked. As the result of some optimistic costing by Sir Bernard Lovell and the main contractor, construction costs for the telescope greatly exceeded the forecasts provided to the treasury. As a result, the public accounts committee censored the treasury and proposals were put forward to make Manchester University foot the bill for the difference. The financial consequences of this for the university were clearly very serious and I proposed on the file that the exchequer should pay. My assistant secretary disagreed. As third secretary, Burke Trend supported my view, but Sir Thomas Padmore, the first secretary, held that in view of the strictures of the public accounts committee a tougher line was needed. Many years later, when the Jodrell Bank telescope was found to be the only instrument that could track signals from certain space-craft, my appreciation of its value was justified.

I was also involved in 'the one that got away', namely Woburn Abbey, when the Duke of Bedford successfully resisted his trustees who wanted to donate the abbey to the country in lieu of death duties.

The most enjoyable aspect of my portfolio was undoubtedly the opportunities it gave me to get out of London and Whitehall. In addition to Woburn Abbey, I visited several other country houses that had been offered in lieu of death duties. I recall particularly well a very pleasant lunch with the Earl of Litchfield's land agent. On one occasion my experience of African land cases influenced my recommendation to my superiors. A beauty spot in Surrey, which had been offered in lieu of death duty, was much sought after by both the National Trust and the Forestry Commission. The merits of the res-pective claims were difficult to assess from the files, so I decided to go and see the situation on the ground. After visiting the site I recommended that the property be divided between the two bodies, a Solomonic judgement that seemed to satisfy all concerned.

On the scientific side I attended as many open days as possible. I learnt about radio carbon dating at the National Physics Laboratory, about shoe design and shoe lasts at the Footwear Research Association and, at the Food Research Association, I learnt why pips in raspberry jam become discoloured.

In London the smoke abatement act was just becoming operative and I enjoyed greatly the opportunity to walk home through the parks at the end of a day's work, through St James's Park, Green Park, Hyde Park and Kensington Gardens. I found I could walk the distance in 55 minutes, 45 of which were through the parks. It was especially enjoyable in the autumn, when the leaves turned brown and the mists created a fairy-tale effect.

On the domestic front, managing three small boys in London provided us with continuing challenges. When we moved in, June immediately contracted some workmen to alter the kitchen to her liking. While the work was in progress she was unable to cook a hot meal for the boys, so she took them upstairs, sat them on the floor in front of a TV set, which the workmen had carried up for her, heated two tins of food over a gas ring and proceeded, with one teaspoon between them, to feed them straight from the tins as they sat open-mouthed in front of the first television they had ever seen. At that moment the local social services health visitor walked in and looked on with obvious disapproval. On a later visit she admired June's new kitchen layout, which was designed to avoid accidents, and later still she asked June to visit some awkward tenants on her behalf. June's most testing encounter was with the Thames Gas Board, which disconnected our gas for alleged non-payment of the bill. Since June knew I had paid it, it was clearly an error on their part, but the local official was unbending and refused to turn it on even after being shown the cheque-book stub as proof of payment. I suggested to June that she write a letter to the *Kensington Post*, but she decided to aim higher and wrote to *The Times*. Much to my surprise her letter was published the next day under the heading 'Turning off the Gas', in the place of honour reserved for droll correspondence. It was some consolation to June when the following day a very senior gas board official drove up to our door in a large Bentley and, after making his apologies, reconnected our gas supply.

On one occasion when June was out in the street surrounded by three children under the age of five, Nicky broke away from her and ran into the road in front of an oncoming taxi. He was saved only by the driver's presence of mind. June apologized, but the driver was clearly shaken and relieved his shock by letting off an extraordinary flow of bad language. 'Oh!' said June, 'You must have been in the navy!' 'How do you know? Were you a Wren?' he asked. 'No, I was a WAAF but the RAF could never touch the navy when it came to swearing!' June thanked him again for stopping in time and they parted on friendly terms.

Over the two years we had a succession of au pairs of many nationalities, recruited through the good offices of a nearby convent hostel in Kensington Square. The sister in charge of the students in the convent came to inspect the flat, June, the children and most of all me before entrusting her girls to us. Our first and best was a Chilean with very high standards who went to parties at the Chilean embassy and informed us that her mother had seven children with a servant for each child. She was followed by an Italian who said 'my father he is reech, I do not like zee 'ousework'. Then came a French one who got on well with the children and planned to go overseas as a missionary, but rarely washed and had an unattractive habit of coming down to breakfast in her housecoat with her hair all over the place. All three were in turn recalled to their countries of origin because a parent fell ill and they were needed at home. Our last au pair was German and so idle that June eventually had to dismiss her, but she refused to leave the comfort of our home. After two weeks June contacted the police who had a set formula for dealing with such situations. A policewoman came round, helped June finish the girl's packing, put her in the car and accompanied them both to a YWCA hostel where she would be closely supervised. The girl's parting shot to June was: 'I learn from you 'ow to manage ze 'usband, yes?'

Although we were in the middle of London, Marloes Road had a village-like atmosphere and its own row of shops. A local barrow boy nicknamed our sons Freckles, Snowball and Ginger, and June made many friends and contacts pushing the pram to and from the primary school. Michael Flanders, the disabled raconteur and singer, lived next door to us in Scarsdale Villas and we could not help but admire the way he was able to lever himself and his wheelchair in and out of his car. We even saw him change a tyre on his car with the 'GNU' number plate that inspired his famous song.

Chris was five by the time we settled in, old enough to go to the Church of England school in Earls Court Road. The buildings were falling apart and the pupils were a very mixed lot socially, with quite a few tough ones, but the school was excellently run and provided a sound grounding. Chris was always sent to school with his lunch money, so we were perplexed in his early days when the form mistress phoned to ask why he had no lunch money with him. She was tactful and kind, explaining that free lunches were available if we could not afford to pay. On questioning Chris, we discovered that he was losing his lunch money playing marbles. We duly cautioned him about the folly of his ways, so were even more perplexed when he started returning from school with more money than he had started out with. We then discovered that not only had he learnt to bet and win at marbles, but that he had also learnt to call in at Woolworths on his way to school to buy marbles at four for a penny, whereas at school they sold for a penny each. It was good early training for an economist and banker.

At weekends in summer we liked getting out of London, so we rented an oast house at Rye from Warren Chetham-Strode, the playwright. This provided us with a valuable safety valve, although returning to London in our little Fiat 600 in heavy traffic on a Sunday evening could be a slow and tedious business, especially since, more often than not, our radiator would boil over.

My secondment finished in early 1960 and we returned to Kenya on a Lloyd Triestino ship from Venice.

We travelled to Venice by train and, as it was crossing the causeway from Mestre into Venice, Chris looked out of the window and, in his best Earls Court Road accent, said: 'Coo er, there's bin a flud 'ere.'

10

Self-Government and Independence

I RETURNED TO KENYA in early 1960 at the beginning of an exciting decade for the country. In November 1959 Patrick Renison had taken over as governor from Evelyn Baring, and Iain Macleod had taken over as secretary of state for the colonies from Alan Lennox-Boyd. The stage was thus set for a constitutional move forward. Macleod paid his first visit to Kenya in the month he was appointed, and after he returned to London the prime minister, Harold Macmillan, decided to call a constitutional conference. It began at Lancaster House in January 1960.

The outcome of the conference was a decision to set up a council of ministers with substantial African representation and a legislative assembly with 65 members, of whom 53 were elected on a common electoral roll. Ten seats were reserved for Europeans, eight for Indians, and two for Arabs. In the ensuing election the Kenya African National Union (KANU) won 19 seats and the Kenya African Democratic Union (KADU) 11. As Kenyatta had not then been released from prison, KANU would not participate in the government, and a KADU government was formed under Ronald Ngala with the support of Michael Blundell's New Kenya Group.

In the treasury I resumed my old post in development planning and as joint secretary of the Cabinet's development committee. This brought me into direct contact with many of the new ministers, including Ronald Ngala, Arap Moi (education), Masinde Muliro (commerce and industry), Michael Blundell (agriculture) and Wilfred Havelock (local government). Intellectually, Blundell stood out, but Arap Moi and Havelock were the most hard-working and thorough of the new ministers. On no occasion did Moi come to a meeting without having first read his papers and done his homework, and I soon realized that both the newspapers and public opinion had underrated him. By contrast, Group-Captain Briggs, a very right-wing member of the committee, went on leave as soon as he was appointed and proved to be a political lightweight.

The new constitution broadened the scope of our overseas financial activities and our financial discussions were no longer confined to the Colonial Office. Kenneth Mackenzie was promoted to the post of minister of finance and development planning, and John Butter, with his innovative and imaginative approach to financing the development plan, became permanent secretary to the treasury. In 1961 the World Bank sent an important economic mission to Kenya to review our economy and I

had the good fortune to be attached to the mission as
liaison officer, while also being promoted to the post of
under secretary in charge of a new division for development finance and development planning.

It was fortunate that at this time the Massachusetts
Institute for Technology (MIT) had just started its
African fellowship programme, and I was lucky to obtain
the services of a very able young economist, Michael
Roemer, to work in the new division. Some years later
when William Clarke, then director of the UK Overseas
Development Institute (ODI), and a member of my
college Oriel, visited Kenya he asked me what could be
the most useful thing the ODI could do to help Kenya, I
replied 'start a British programme for outstanding
graduates like that of MIT.' He took my advice and,
obtaining support from the government and from several
foundations, he started the highly successful ODI
'Fellows in Africa' programme. I was pleased therefore
when, several years later, our eldest son Christopher was
awarded a fellowship under this programme to work for
two years with the Lesotho Development Corporation.

Jomo Kenyatta was released from detention in August
1961, shortly after Duncan Sandys was appointed
secretary of state for the colonies. Sandys immediately
convened another constitutional conference, this time at
Lancaster House in London in 1962. It resulted in more
African representation and a second chamber to provide
theoretical safeguards for minorities. It also led to the
setting up of a ministry of settlement, with a million-acre

settlement scheme to buy out European farms at a cost of £15 million. A KADU/KANU coalition government was formed with Ronald Ngala as minister of state for administration and Jomo Kenyatta as minister of state for economic planning. Bruce McKenzie became minister for settlement, Michael Blundell retained agriculture, Tom Mboya became minister for labour, and James Gichuru became minister for finance. My position as a result became rather schizophrenic, for I had to work to Jomo Kenyatta and his permanent secretary Donald Baron on economic planning matters, but to Frank Gilboy and John Butter on finance and foreign aid.

It was an interesting experience to work near Kenyatta, who had an excellent relationship with Baron. He was both a showman and very astute. He could be charming, yet at the same time would leave me with a feeling of something more sinister underneath. He was wise and cunning, and had an underlying liking and respect for the British. This I attribute largely to three people – Oscar Watkins, who had been his adviser and interpreter when he gave evidence to the Hilton Young Commission in 1927; his English wife Edna; and Leslie Whitehouse, who had been his 'gaoler' when he was interned in Turkana during Mau Mau.

Under the KANU/KADU government I undertook quite a lot of foreign travel on foreign aid missions and in London there were routine negotiations with the Colonial Office. The most interesting mission, however, was to Washington where, with three ministers – James Gichuru (finance), Tom Mboya (labour) and Masinde Muliro (commerce and industry) – I visited the World Bank and USAID. Mboya, who was clearly the brains behind the mission, had his own contacts, many of which he had obviously made in the days of a student airlift he had organized to the USA. On arriving in Washington he asked me to contact a student friend of his, Washington Okumu, whom I duly found sitting in a suite at the Mayflower Hotel eating oysters and surrounded by a bevy of beautiful black damsels. I explained our mission and he said he could put in a good word for us with President Kennedy. I was surprised that he should have such high-level contacts, and even more so when I met him again a few days later and he said: 'I saw Kennedy on Saturday and he said that your mission will get a sympathetic hearing.' I was sceptical of his story so phoned the colonial attaché at the British embassy and asked if he could find out where Kennedy had spent Saturday and who had seen him. He assured me that he could and a few hours later he phoned me back to say that Kennedy had spent Saturday yachting at Hyannis Port, that no one had seen him and that he could find no such name as Okumu in the White House book for that week. Anyhow, we did get a sympathetic hearing at both the World Bank and USAID, and the mission was considered a success.

It was our wedding anniversary while we were in Washington, so I phoned June in Nairobi. It was a good line and she was delighted to hear from me. When there were no pips at the end of three minutes I thought the operator was being kind to us, for she had heard me saying it was our anniversary, so we went on talking for about eight minutes. When I got my hotel bill I discovered that the phone call had cost me more than my accommodation for the whole week.

June had her hands more than full at this time, for our son Jonathan had been born in March 1961 in Mrs Catchpole's nursing home in Nairobi, and she now had four small boys at home. He had been a particularly large baby, so large indeed that until he was born the doctor had thought that there might be twins on the way. At six foot four he is now the tallest of our sons. Not only was the idea of five sons and the domestic rearrangements that would entail rather daunting, but Kenya income tax law at that time only provided a tax allowance for a maximum of four children.

In 1962 I went to Addis Ababa as joint Kenya delegate to a conference of the Economic Commission for Africa. That visit turned out to be very important for two fortuitous reasons. First, I met Christopher Eckenstein, who was then special assistant to the secretary general of the United Nations Conference on Trade and Development (UNCTAD). Eckenstein heard me speaking and liked my approach to economic cooperation. I had not even heard of UNCTAD at the time, but that encounter was to establish my career after I left Kenya. Second, I met Sir Oliver Wright, the British ambassador to Ethiopia at a cocktail party. I mentioned to him that I had been asked to talent spot for a new Kenya foreign service. He immediately introduced me to Robert Ouko, who was then head of the Kenya students group at Addis Ababa university, giving him a very strong recommendation. I passed this on when I got back to Nairobi and in due course Robert joined the new Kenya foreign service. He never looked back and rose to ministerial rank after a distinguished career in the Kenya administration. He was sadly murdered in mysterious circumstances while in office as minister for foreign affairs.

Malcolm Macdonald replaced Patrick Renison as governor at the end of 1962, and in May 1963 more elections were held. These ushered in a period of self-government under a KANU government, with Kenyatta as prime minister, Oginga Odinga as deputy prime minister, Gichuru in finance and economic planning, and McKenzie in agriculture and settlement.

By this time I had become quite an expert on foreign aid and joined a Kenya ministerial delegation to the Organization for Economic Cooperation and Development (OECD) development assistance committee in Paris. These meetings did not lead to much, though we consumed some excellent food and wine in the OECD restaurant, and I was able to lunch one day with Peter Ady, my former tutor at St Anne's College, who was at that time working at the OECD.

Another result of my acquired expertise was that I was invited to give a paper at a Cambridge University summer school on 'Planning the Receipt of Aid'. I was put up as a counterpoise to John White of the Overseas Development

Institute (ODI) who had become an expert on aid donors. By this time Kenya had been outstandingly successful in obtaining aid. Our annual receipts from aid equalled £14 per head of the population, the highest of any developing country in the world.

As a result of my success in obtaining aid I was awarded the OBE. The citation read:

> Throughout his fifteen years service Mr Knowles has maintained a remarkable degree of enthusiasm and efficiency in carrying out his duties. He has been largely responsible for the success of the Government's efforts in obtaining aid for development from international organizations and overseas governments. He has applied his considerable constructive abilities and great energy unstintingly to the service of the Government, and the constructive nature of his mind has helped to put in practical form the plans put up by various Ministries.

In December 1964 Kenya became a republic. Malcolm McDonald ceased to be governor general and became the UK high commissioner; Kenyatta became president and Odinga became vice-president. From that point onwards Kenya civil servants became ineligible for British decorations as a reward for Kenya government service.

Both immediately before, and just after independence the volume of foreign aid work developed rapidly as countries from both the West and East fell over each other to send missions and to open embassies. Every embassy had to celebrate its national day, as well as visits by VIPs and aid missions. For those Kenya officials dealing with financial aid and technical assistance there was soon hardly a day without at least one cocktail party; sometimes there would be two or even three that protocol required one to attend. One of my assistants, Terence Libby, who was dealing with technical assistance, acquired so many invitations in one year that he covered a wall with them.

There were I regret to say certain 'spin-off benefits' from my post, and I had to distinguish carefully between those that could be accepted without compromising the concept of 'pecuniary interest', which governed all colonial service officers, and those that went too far. Once when I did take advantage of my position was when my niece Caroline wanted to marry an Italian engineer working on the Italian San Marco rocket project at Ngomeni. He was due to leave Kenya at the end of the year and they had about three months to complete the very considerable amount of red tape and paperwork that Italian bureaucracy required. This included a certificate of 'no impediment' and evidence that she had no communist affiliations. The Italian consul happily accepted my assurance that she was not a communist, but the production of a certificate of 'no impediment' presented more of a problem because the UK refused to issue such certificates. However, as she had dual Kenya/UK citizenship at the time I was able to persuade the registrar-general, David Coward, to design one for Kenya and issue one for £20 as a revenue-earning activity. As he had received several other similar requests he was happy to do so. The bridegroom's father completed the good work by leaving bottles of whisky at the appropriate government departments in Rome to ensure that the file kept moving, and the necessary formalities were completed in time for a wedding in Kenya at the end of the year.

The wide range of foreign aid missions provided added interest. The strong mission the West Germans sent to the independence celebrations included Claus von Amsberg, the diplomat who later married the heir to the Dutch throne. One member of the Swiss technical assistance mission remarked that the facilities at the Nairobi technical college compared favourably with any in Switzerland, but then went on to say: 'what a wonderful country for our young doctors. You have every disease a doctor could hope to find and it will not matter too much if he loses a few patients.'

The Chinese sent a strong trade mission as part of their quest for influence in Africa. Their embassy threw a large party for the mission but it was unclear from the invitations whether or not wives were invited. I decided to take June with me, but as we entered the embassy driveway I realized that it was indeed meant to be a stag party. I hastily tried to back our car out of the drive, but a Chinese official spotted me and insisted that June should join the party, along with an African lady who had made the same mistake.

Not long after that party Kenya decided to send a
mission to China under the leadership of Vice-President
Oginga Odinga. As the main object of the mission was to
seek aid, I managed to brief and attach one of our young
treasury officers, John Matere Keriri, to it. While teaching
at the University of Nairobi, June had spotted John as a
particularly good economics graduate and had suggested
we recruit him to the treasury. When they arrived in
China and Odinga asked John what he thought they
should ask the Chinese to give them, he replied: 'Tell
them we need a million pounds to nationalize the Kenya
Broadcasting Corporation.' Odinga did so and in due
course we received a million pounds, paid in sterling
without strings, in two equal instalments through London. We did not, I regret, tell the Chinese that the KBC
was practically bankrupt and that we expected in any case
to have to take it over.

Given that we were on the constant lookout for new
talent at this time, when Washington Okumu came on
leave to Kenya after our mission to the USA, and performed a holiday job in the treasury to our satisfaction, I
asked him if he would be interested in a post of assistant
secretary in the treasury when he completed his studies
in the USA. He replied that he was considering applying
for the professorial chair of economics at the University
of Nairobi, which might be becoming vacant. I retired
from the competition. I subsequently heard he had taken
a job with the East African Railways and Harbours
(EAR&H) but then somehow managed to get detained on

Manda Island. His ambition to become an economics professor was fulfilled some years later and I believe he played an important role in persuading the Zulus in South Africa to join the ANC government.

A minor government reshuffle accompanied the declaration of a republic in December 1964 when the economic planning ministerial portfolio was separated from finance. James Gichuru remained in charge of finance, but Tom Mboya was appointed minister for economic planning. His first move was to recruit a team of American advisers from the Ford Foundation, led by Professor Edgar Edwards from Rice University in Texas. I became deputy director of planning in the new ministry and had to work with the new team. At first I found the arrangement rather uncomfortable. I felt eased out, and was given the impression that they found me a nuisance with no experience of planning. However, we soon learnt to respect each other's qualities and worked well together to produce, first a sessional paper on African socialism, and then a new development plan. Though I contributed to its contents, the sessional paper was largely the work of Edwards and it was a brilliant piece of drafting. There was an urgent need to create an African middle class to help run a stable society. However, socialist philosophies were very popular in Africa at that time, particularly in Tanzania, and Kenyatta's position in relation to Odinga was at the time a delicate one, so we had to adjust to the way the wind was blowing. Hence, Sessional Paper no. 10 on African socialism was produced, which was in fact a blueprint for a form of African capitalism. It became known as *The Little Red Book*.

About this time, with the cold war in full swing, I was involved in a little incident that may have changed the course of Kenya history. Because June had been teaching at the College of Social Studies at Kikuyu, we were invited to attend the passing out day at a new adult education college Odinga had established with Russian financial support. It was called the Lumumba Institute and there was a strong representation of East European diplomats to mark the occasion; in fact the only faces from the West that I recognized were those of the Swedish ambassador and his wife. It was clear from the proceedings that not only had the students attending the college been heavily indoctrinated, but also that the KANU officials who had attended the course would be returning to their districts just when senior KANU officials would be at a conference in Nairobi. There was therefore every chance that the way could be opened for a left-wing takeover of the KANU district offices. I reported this possibility to the appropriate quarters and heard no more, but there was no *coup d'état*.

In 1965 John Butter went on leave and John Michuki replaced him as permanent secretary for finance. I was promoted to Michuki's post of deputy secretary for finance. John Butter subsequently returned from leave as an adviser. We also had a new adviser, Michael Stewart, whom Harold Wilson had offered to Kenyatta and who was married to the daughter of Nicholas Kaldor, the famous Cambridge economist. He struck me as a rather confident young man who knew all the answers, and it was not long before he and Butter were no longer on speaking terms.

As deputy secretary I became very involved in East African matters. In June 1965 Nyerere, Obote and Kenyatta pledged to work for a political federation of East Africa, but showed no willingness to surrender sovereignty. Following his defeat in Kenya European politics, Vasey went to Tanzania as minister for finance. There he backed the Blumenthal report for Tanzania on monetary management and broke up the East African Currency Board. There was, however, a willingness to maintain a form of common market, and to keep common services, provided that terms satisfactory to all could be negotiated. A commission was therefore proposed to look into the relevant issues. Kenya suggested a distinguished Australian as chairman, but Tanzania would not hear of a chairman from a Commonwealth country. Tanzania in turn suggested a Dutch chairman, but in view of the Dutch royal family's farm holdings in Tanzania, Kenya felt he might be too pro-Tanzania.

About this time I chanced to see a cable from UN New York saying that Professor Kjeld Philip was available for some UN technical assistance assignments. His CV seemed perfect for the East African Commission of Inquiry. He was a Danish citizen, had been professor of economics at a Swedish university and then, in his own country, had been successively minister of finance, planning and commerce. The problem was how to get him chosen. With my assistance, Bernard Chidzero, a very successful UNDP resident representative, concocted a little plot. When I asked him one day for the secret of his success, he replied: 'I look at a ministry and ask myself who in the ministry does the work? Then I ring that person up.'

We decided to cook up a technical assistance mission for Philip to go to Lusaka at a time when a projected conference on African cooperation and development was scheduled to take place. At the same time we briefed Mboya and McKenzie to introduce Philip to the other ministers from Tanzania and Uganda. This was duly done and Philip was accepted as the ideal candidate.

He came back to Nairobi with Chidzero to discuss the terms of his contract and phoned his wife to tell her about his proposed assignment. She objected on the grounds that she would not see him for the next six months and urged him to turn the assignment down. Chidzero came to see me looking very glum. Fortunately, the Danish ambassador in Nairobi owed me a good turn for helping to save one of his dinner parties from disaster when he was hosting a party for some of Denmark's leading industrialists, the Mollers. The ambassador agreed to help when I pointed out that for the good name of Denmark Professor Philip should take on the East African assignment. He contacted his foreign office, which leant on Professor Philip to accept, and the commission was able to start work.

24. Nick, Johnny, Chris and Mark, Nairobi.

I occasionally had to handle air traffic rights and the related subject of landing charges. In 1963 we had a visit from some senior executives from Pan American Airways, which was opening up a new route to Nairobi from the USA via the west coast of Africa, and also planning to build an Intercontinental Hotel in Nairobi. There were some difficult negotiations about the hotel, but a ceremonial dinner to commemorate the opening of the new route had to be cancelled when Juan Trippe and all the Pan American Airways visitors were laid low with stomach upsets.

Air traffic rights fell under the jurisdiction of the East African Community (EAC), and our ministry of transport represented Kenya in most of its negotiations. Kenya

usually came off badly. Most airlines wanted traffic rights
at Nairobi and those that already had them were reluctant
to grant them to newcomers. Our representatives were
usually forced into agreeing to the compromise position
of granting rights to Nairobi only if an airline was prepared to land in Dar es Salaam and Entebbe as well. This
had an adverse effect on our tourism and air freight
exports. Planes would fly north through Nairobi with
empty holds while Kenya fruit and vegetables rotted at
the airport waiting authorized northbound capacity to
Europe. So long as the EAC existed as a viable body it was
a difficult situation to change, but as it broke up we started
to take unilateral action through presidential orders.

Airlines always resisted increases in landing charges
and instead tried to persuade us to impose passenger
airport taxes, which of course they could pass on to the
traveller. As the demand for landing rights in Nairobi
exceeded the supply of places, we were in a strong
position to increase landing charges, since increased
charges did not affect the willingness of airlines to come
to Nairobi. Passenger airport taxes were, quite apart from
the nuisance of collecting them, a strong disincentive to
tourists. I therefore resisted such charges and stated our
position at two International Civil Aviation Organization
(ICAO) conferences in Montreal. However, when I left
the treasury the airlines got their way.

One responsibility of the development finance division
was to make investments on behalf of the National Provident Fund, which had been set up to try and start some

kind of pension scheme for Kenyans and to relieve the burden on their extended families when they could no longer work. Normally, most of the money was invested in local issues of Kenya government stock. There was no reason, however, why we should not invest in suitable equities if and when they became available. We spotted that East Africa Power and Lighting shares had fallen as low as 14 shillings in London following the nationalization in Tanzania, which had taken place at the original issue price of 20 shillings. This was an obvious bargain and we started buying in London on behalf of the Provident Fund, using several brokers to disguise the source of the buying. Over a period of several months we were able to buy a considerable quantity of shares at well below the issue price without the market waking up to what we were doing.

In the first part of 1967 I learnt that President Kenyatta had appointed me secretary of a commission of inquiry into the maize industry, of which the chairman would be Mr Justice Chanan Singh. This was a surprise to me and I first heard the news on Kenya radio on a Sunday evening. I was of course aware that there were near famine conditions in Ukambani and that the *Daily Nation*, whose editor was a former private secretary of Kenyatta, had been campaigning for such an inquiry for several weeks. It was rumoured that the minister for marketing, Paul Ngei, and his wife Emma, who ran a shop called Emma's Stores, were profiteering from the sale of famine relief maize.

I was told that evidence should be taken in public and one of the best police inspectors, Tony Cross, was made available to lead the investigations and marshal the facts. The inquiry was a three-week 'wonder', commanding the headlines in the press nearly every day as the story unfolded. According to the press reports, Emma remained listening throughout, changing her dress twice daily. Only once did we go into secret session. This was after lunch one day when the minister for works, who had obviously lunched too well, found it difficult to stand up straight in the witness box. The chairman then dismissed the journalists and put the inquiry into secret session. Rather desperately he then said: 'Remember Mr X that you are a minister of the government', at which point the minister held the sides of the witness box very firmly and gave evidence in a rather thick voice.

The chairman drafted most of our report, which included one chapter entitled 'Alice in Wonderland'. Fearing there night be an attempt to suppress it after publication, I sent a few advance copies to an Oxford academic friend for the benefit of posterity.

There were in fact attempts to suppress it, but pressures to publish could not be resisted. The president's office, however, did manage to release the report on a day when there was another big news story, and it attracted less publicity than it might have done. The president did nothing with the report, though I felt he should have sacked two ministers, including Paul Ngei, the minister for Marketing. I believe that the president was badly advised and was told that if he sacked Ngei, a Mkamba, he would have trouble from the Kamba people, from among whom a large number of police and army personnel were recruited. In Machakos, Ngei led a group known as Kanu A. My belief was that if he had been sacked, Kanu B in Machakos, which had some influential leaders, would have taken its place and there would have been no trouble with the services. When Kenyatta refused to sack Ngei I wanted to resign from government service as a protest, but John Butter discouraged me and I took no action.

Later in 1967, John Michuki went on leave and I was made acting permanent secretary to the ministry of finance and expected to hold the appointment for about six months. Shortly after my appointment I learnt that Kenya Toray Mills was in financial difficulties and had applied to the ministry to grant it a duty drawback on all imports of synthetic fibre from Japan. I was suspicious of this application and asked if we could see the accounts. The firm agreed immediately and I sent a treasury adviser to examine them. Within 24 hours he informed me that the main cause of its problems was that Kenya Toray Mills was paying a large concealed commission on imports of fibre to a front company owned by the minister of commerce, Dr Julius Kiano, and his wife. I therefore sent for the two Japanese directors and informed them that so long as they were paying this commission I could not recommend a drawback, but that if they were prepared to provide signed affidavits about the commission payments I would be prepared to consider making a recommendation that drawbacks be granted. They provided signed affidavits and I passed these to the heads of the CID who put one of his best inspectors onto the case. A full dossier was prepared and sent to the attorney general, Charles Njonjo. My disappointment can be imagined when the attorney general gave a *nolle prosequi* decision.

While I was acting permanent secretary the Bank of England, through our central bank, tipped us off about an impending sterling devaluation; so as to give us a chance to move some of our reserves into other currencies. We were in a dangerous position because we were holding all our reserves in sterling, while maintaining US dollar parity. To buy other currencies I needed the approval of the governor of our central bank, Duncan Ndegwa, who was away playing golf somewhere north of Mount Kenya and could not be contacted. In view of our expanding trade with Japan I would have liked to hold some of our reserves in yen while keeping the greater part in US dollars. The situation was getting desperate when, about an hour before the deadline, I managed to contact Duncan on a very bad telephone line. I could not persuade him to buy yen, but he agreed to move our reserves into dollars.

My term as acting permanent secretary came to a sudden end when I collapsed unexpectedly one afternoon at a meeting in the Central Bank of Kenya. The doctors suspected a stroke, so I was given sick leave and John

Michuki was recalled to take up his post. I was duly sent to see a Harley Street specialist, Dr Roger Bannister, who was famous for being the first man to run a four-minute mile. He decided that my problem was overwork and that I needed a good rest. So we went on holiday to Austria where, since I was still not feeling at all well, I went to see another doctor. He immediately diagnosed the cause of the problem. A disc in my neck, which I had damaged while playing rugby many years earlier, had moved into a position where it was pressing on a nerve and interrupting the blood supply to my head. An Austrian chiropractor, who was an ex-boxer, rapidly manipulated it back into position.

When I returned from leave I did not want to go back to the treasury, so was seconded for common market duties with the Ministry of Commerce and Industry (which now had a new minister). Apart from representing Kenya on the East African Tariff Advisory Committee, I was chairman of the Kenya Duty Drawbacks Committee. In the latter role my favourite case will always be that of the Kenya fly fishing industry where, by granting a rebate on imported hooks, we enabled a small industry to grow and take a large share of the world market for dry flies, selling even to Woolworth's stores. This was a cottage industry that a mother had started on a farm to occupy her handicapped son. The farm labourers had then joined in and were earning some useful extra money by tying flies in their spare time.

My biggest success in the East African Tariff Advisory

Committee was to negotiate a tariff concession for the Kenya paper industry in return for Kenya keeping out of tyre production. This negotiating success was, however, thrown away when the minister for finance allowed a tyre factory to start in Kenya. This was not at first very successful and proved to be a drag on the economy.

At the end of 1968 I decided to resign and prepared to leave Kenya in early 1969. I was given a very good farewell party in the treasury and everything went very well until, in my farewell speech, I touched on the delicate subject of corruption and expressed the hope that the government 'code of pecuniary interest' would continue to be observed. There was an embarrassing silence. The code was in fact thrown out of the window in 1971 when the government accepted the Ndegwa report recommendation (Report of the Commission of Inquiry (Public Service Structure and Remuneration) 1970–71) that civil servants should be allowed to have business interests.

11

Life in Geneva and France

W HEN I WAS considering leaving Kenya in 1968, Glasgow University had already approached me with an offer of a research fellowship in economic cooperation and development, and June had been offered a teaching post in economics. On our last night in Kenya, while sitting on packing cases in our house and eating supper out of a sardine tin, we had a visit from Christopher Eckenstein of UNCTAD. He had come straight from an ECA (UN Economic Commission for Africa) conference in Addis Ababa, where he had met Arvind Barve of the Ministry of Commerce and Industry who had told him that I was leaving Kenya. He recalled having heard me speak at the ECA in 1962 and wanted to know if I might be interested in taking up an appointment at UNCTAD as an interregional adviser on economic cooperation between developing countries, for which a new post had been established following the latest UNCTAD meeting in New Delhi.

I was not ready for his approach. I told him that I had tentative plans to go to Glasgow and that in the meanwhile I intended to take a long holiday with my family in

Austria to do some skiing. At this point he suggested I take a side trip to Geneva from Austria for a talk. After about a month in Austria and having heard nothing further from Glasgow, I went over to Geneva and met Eckenstein in the Palais des Nations. He asked me to pay a call on the secretary general of UNCTAD, Manuel Perrez-Guerrero, who greeted me by saying that he was delighted to hear I was coming to work for UNCTAD. I said this was a little premature but that I had the matter under consideration. Eckenstein then suggested that, since I did not expect to go to Glasgow until the following year, I take a six-month contract with UNCTAD to fill in some of the time. I agreed to do this and we moved to Geneva in June 1969.

We immediately ran into currency, exchange-control and accommodation problems. We had been unable to move any of our capital from Kenya when we left and, being unaware of quite how high Swiss prices were, I had made the mistake of asking the Bank of England for too little Swiss currency when we went to Geneva. It was, however, mid-summer and we had brought our camping trailer from Austria, so we parked it at a camping ground at Point de la Bise by the lake and the boys lived there during the school holiday, commuting in by bus for breakfast, first to a small furnished studio we rented in the centre of Geneva in the Place des Alpes, and then to a somewhat larger furnished apartment in the Residence Cavalieri in the Rue de Lausanne.

We remained in Cavalieri throughout the hot summer

of 1969. Our main excitement there was when Johnny looked out of our door one morning and said: 'There's a dead man on the mat.' I took a look and there was indeed a man lying there, but the strong smell of alcohol on his breath suggested he was not dead. I phoned the police and two constables arrived quickly in a small Volkswagen. One immediately pushed his fingers up the man's nostrils, whereupon he stood up shakily, saluted and walked downstairs. We learnt afterwards from the young women in the adjacent apartment that he had followed one of them upstairs the previous evening and had obviously spent the night on our doormat.

At a meeting about a month later I heard a man behind me saying he had received a sudden posting to Africa and would be giving up his house in Chambesy. I turned to him and said I would be interested if the rent was acceptable. He told me it was 650 Swiss francs a month, which was very low for Geneva, and that if I were interested I should look at the house immediately because others were also interested and he needed to find a tenant right away. On viewing it, I found it to be the most curiously inconvenient house I had seen for a long time, but it was situated in a nice garden in a quiet cul-de-sac and it was most unlikely that I would find anything comparable within my means. I therefore agreed to take it without consulting June and we were able to move from Point de la Bise and the Rue de Lausanne.

Soon afterwards I was sent on a mission to Turkey, so had to leave June alone to face the problems of living in

Chambesy in particular and Switzerland in general. At this time women did not have the vote in Geneva, and the Swiss disapproved of women doing anything as unfeminine as operating a bank account or dealing with officialdom. She had difficulty first with cashing cheques on our bank account, even though she was specifically authorized to do so, then with importing a small sailing dinghy through customs and registering it with the *Service de Navigation* for Lac Leman. When they asked her why 'Monsieur' was not doing it, she told them that it was a 'pram' dinghy and that in England the women pushed the prams.

We discovered that the Swiss had a dry sense of humour shortly after arriving in Chambesy. The first time June decided to take the train from Geneva to Chambesy, which was the next station on the line, she did not know to which booking office at the large Gare de Cornavin she should go for her ticket and inadvertently went to the one reserved for international journeys. With a straight face the ticket clerk issued her the ticket and said 'Bon voyage, Madame.' It took her several minutes to understand the joke. The Swiss could also laugh at themselves, as we found when we went to see the film *The Swiss Makers* about the trials and tribulations of becoming a Swiss citizen. There was even a local joke of the Englishman, Irishman and Scotsman variety, but with a Genevois, Bernois and Vaudois.

As foreigners, we came under the scrutiny of the *contrôle d'habitants*, whose inspector would periodically come round to our house to see that we were behaving like good citizens. We learnt that unless our front hedge was cut by a certain date in July, the commune would cut it at our expense. We found that there were other 'interdictions', for example when washing could be put out to dry. And I learnt about *responsabilité civile* (civil liability) insurance. When I asked why this was necessary I was told that it would cover me if my boys broke a neighbour's window with an arrow or catapult. I did in fact make a small claim under this policy several years later when a woman whom June had accidentally touched with an oar at the UN *plage* sued me for the cost of a course of physiotherapy.

Our neighbours on one side were an elderly couple from Berne and because they came from another canton they too were classed as foreigners (*étrangers*). It interested us that when the old man fell down in their garden and could not get up, it was to us that the old lady came for help and not to their Genevois neighbours on the other side.

The Swiss have some very good points. They are, as is well known, very hard-working. They are also early risers and it is the only country in which I have ever been given a dentist's appointment at 6.30 on a Saturday morning. However, we found their insistence that everything in Switzerland was wonderful rather hypocritical and suggestive instead that they pushed difficult problems out of sight and discouraged open discussion in public and in the press. There was undoubtedly some corruption and several *scandale*s erupted while we were there, including one of an official found running a brothel in Geneva. The greatest *scandale* perhaps was the escape from Geneva gaol of the financier Licio Gelli who was on remand there for his part in the Italian Masonic lodge P2 scandal. To their credit Geneva university students put on a thinly veiled musical satire about the event. The Bernie Cornfeld fund of funds débâcle also reflected no credit on the Swiss when Cornfeld was charged only with respect to the few Swiss citizens who lost money through his enterprise.

At a domestic level we encountered a problem when Chris was working as a driver/courier in the holidays and was required to work dangerously long hours, which obviously contravened the labour regulations for safe driving. We worried that he might have an accident through fatigue and told him to make representations to his employers. When they refused to shorten his hours, he said 'what would happen if I went to the police and said that you were breaking the labour laws?' They replied 'we would see that you never got another job in Geneva.' It was not a good country in which to be poor. While in Chambesy we had a cleaner whose husband died after a long illness, leaving her with very little money and no form of public assistance. Eventually, to his credit, the owner of our estate agency (*régie*) helped her to get a local authority flat.

The meticulous nature of the Swiss led to very precise timekeeping. Trains ran almost to the minute and we would see guests for supper drive up to our gate a few minutes early and sit in their cars until the precise hour of the invitation arrived. But such attention to detail could also have its down side. One day Johnny, who was only nine at the time, was travelling on a bus in Geneva and he omitted to get his ticket stamped properly in the appropriate machine. An inspector arrested him and, telephoning June, asked her if she had a son whose hair was too long. When she replied that she had four, he gave her a lecture on the seriousness of Johnny's offence and the need to train one's children properly. The only result was that Johnny refused to travel alone on a bus in Geneva again.

In our early days it was possible for foreign students to get holiday jobs in Switzerland. Chris, for example, who had passed his advanced driver's test, worked for a travel firm for several seasons and became one of its most sought after drivers. He was given important English-speaking visitors like Colonel Sanders of the Kentucky Fried Chicken chain, and Tommy Steele the pop star. Nick got a job with a computer software company and was reported to be the only software consultant to qualify for a 'youth fare' air ticket. Mark got a job in a co-op supermarket, which he lost after sticking white wine price labels onto champagne bottles! Julia, then Chris's fiancée, got a job in the meat department of the same co-op and was put to work updating the 'best before' labels on the meat packages.

When the UK joined the EEC five years after we

arrived in Geneva we decided to move to France. This offered a number of advantages over living in Switzerland, and the frontier ran right up to Geneva airport, so passengers had the option of exiting into either Switzerland or France. The part of France just beyond the airport, the Pays de Gex, was a duty-free zone, an historical survival from the Congress of Vienna, following which the canton of Geneva had been joined to the rest of Switzerland. The zone was in fact only duty free for certain products such as butter, where it lay outside the EEC 'butter mountain', or for non-EEC cars such as Ladas.

The main advantage of France was that accommodation there was much cheaper than in Geneva and we could afford to buy a house. We found an old farmhouse that required modernizing and redecorating in the commune of Ornex. June soon had our boys helping to redecorate it as a summer holiday task. They crossed over from Switzerland every day and with their overalls bedaubed with paint became well known to the local Swiss customs officers, one of whom one day commented 'I see that today you are painting the blue bedroom, Madame.'

Our house was in fact less than a kilometre from the frontier where there was a secondary border crossing that the Swiss customs seldom manned. Given that our new house had a very large wine cellar, it was quite possible that former farm owners had smuggled wine into Switzerland as a sideline. On one occasion when June took a considerable quantity of wine from France into Switzerland to celebrate the opening of a new church, the Swiss customs officer, who was a good Catholic, opened the car boot, which was full of wine, and said: 'I can't see anything dutiable there, Madame,' and shut it again.

Life in France was much more relaxed than in Switzerland and there was no *service des étrangers* watching over everything we did. When June had to go and see the French customs, instead of asking 'where is Monsieur?' as in Switzerland, the customs officer said 'Can't you forge your husband's signature?' In Ferney-Voltaire, only a kilometre from the border, drivers happily parked in the middle of the road, whereas cars abandoned in a snowstorm in Geneva were served with parking tickets. In Ornex, provided you took out your house insurance with the mayor, who was an insurance agent, bureaucracy was seldom a problem.

The only time I had a problem was when I met our son Nick on the Swiss side of Geneva airport one morning and, since I was in a hurry to get to the office, I decided to go through the local unmanned customs post to avoid the queue at the main frontier post. As luck would have it, on that particular morning France had sent its *brigade mobile* to man this post and Nick's baggage was thoroughly searched. I had asked him to bring back a supply of powdered vitamins for me and it took some time to persuade the French customs that Nick, who at that time had very long hair, was not smuggling cocaine.

We lived happily in France for ten years, during which

time our house became a staging post for friends and relatives travelling through Europe. When some American
friends came to see us, driving a petrol-consuming car,
they asked the local filling station to fill the car up with
'gas'. Since *gas-oil* is the French word for diesel, that was
what they were given and they then had to get their tank
drained. Our son Johnny decided to take a sabbatical year
between school and university and spent the autumn
helping with the Beaujolais wine harvest. He spent the
winter working in a ski shop in a leading ski resort,
where he learnt a lot about human nature as well as
greatly improving his skiing. We stayed on in France for
about 18 months after I retired, taking the opportunity to
tour round Europe as much as possible. After we sold our
French house we spent a long retirement holiday in
Austria and then, in 1983, moved to England.

When I retired we had, except for two years in London
in the 1950s, lived outside England for nearly 35 years.
We had no common roots except for our time at Oxford,
which we had both loved. After searching unsuccessfully
for a house in Oxford that we both liked and could
afford, we looked at some smaller towns on the London
side of the city, for we then had two sons living in London. Our requirement was a small town with the basic
services needed in old age – a doctor, pharmacy, dentist,
bank and supermarket, plus a bus service into Oxford for
when we could no longer drive. This we found in Watlington.

While serving in India and Burma I became interested

in Eastern religions and in studying comparative religion. As a district officer in Kenya I also become interested in the many splinter churches and why they had split from the main Christian denominations. I tried to get Sir Alister Hardy, then president of Manchester College, Oxford, interested and he in turn interested me in research into religious experience. Shortly after I retired I was approached to become a trustee and treasurer of the Alister Hardy Trust for research into religious experience, which was then in Oxford. I remained a trustee until the trust and research centre moved to the University of Wales at Lampeter 20 years later. The trust has since extended its activities to include research in China, Russia and India, in addition to its existing research programme in Britain.

12

Working for the UN

WORKING FOR the UN was a very different experience from working for the Kenya government, both administratively and politically. When I first joined it took me six months to get a regular pay cheque and I lived off a series of cash advances. I thought at first that I had come to work for a banana republic. The weaknesses in the system were partly due to the system of financing, which was based on funding specific programmes.

There was inevitably some duplication, as well as competition for the available money and work, particularly between the regional economic commissions, and Geneva, New York and Vienna. The regional commissions used the argument that those in the region knew what was best for the region, the Economic Commission for Africa (ECA) being particularly fond of this argument. New York, Geneva and Vienna were able, however, to command a wider and more qualified range of staff and experts.

I was a rather slow learner in the ways of UN political in-fighting. This placed me at a considerable disadvantage when I was promoted suddenly to be the acting director of a division and found myself exposed to Latin-American political intrigues about which I was almost completely ignorant. I was a technician not a politician, so I was very happy when after three months a substantive appointment was made and I could go back to my substantive advisory job, which carried the same pay as the directorship. I also learnt during my acting directorship that there were clear limits to the director's powers, which to an outsider looked much greater than they were in practice. On the other hand, the splendid setting of the Palais des Nations, which had been the headquarters of the old League of Nations in the interwar years, gave the impression that its occupants belonged to a very powerful organization, an impression that the splendour of some of the rooms and certain luxurious facilities such as the top-floor restaurant merely strengthened.

The UN at that time provided yet another arena in which the cold war and other global and regional conflicts were played out. National competition for key UN posts was a reflection of that situation and some countries would go to great lengths to get one of their nationals into a particular post. Then, once installed in such posts, they would lean quite heavily on them. In my experience at least, the UK was a notable exception to this practice, for not only did it never lean on me, but I could hardly persuade it to take any interest in what I did, even when some small national interest was at stake.

It was also obvious that the Palais des Nations was at

that time an active front for various intelligence services, some of which tried to dominate the UN staff association. There appeared to be a gentlemen's agreement about certain posts. I became personally aware of the extent of the intelligence activity when I came into my office early one Monday morning to find a photograph of my eldest son, which I had left in one of my desk drawers, lying on the floor under the photocopying machine. I could only infer that someone copying papers from my drawer had dropped it.

I worked for UNCTAD (the United Nations Conference on Trade and Development) from 1969 until 1984. From 1969 to 1980 I was employed as an interregional adviser on economic cooperation among developing countries, from 1980 to 1982 as senior adviser to ECOWAS (Economic Community of West African States), and from 1982 to 1984 as a consultant to ECOWAS.

My post of interregional adviser was created as the result of a resolution passed at the New Delhi UNCTAD, where the emphasis was placed on Third World countries helping themselves and where some rather optimistic hopes were expressed about what might be achieved. The development of this particular UNCTAD programme was largely the work of Christopher Eckenstein. He was a visionary and when he died a few years later he donated his entire estate to starting up a Swiss foundation to help the Third World.

My first assignment was to join an advisory mission to

advise the RCD (Regional Commission for Development) countries of Iran, Pakistan and Turkey on methods of extending economic cooperation under the RCD cooperation agreement they had concluded. There was a central secretariat in Teheran. Eckenstein led the mission, which was primarily concerned with looking at trade preferences and trade cooperation. As a corollary of trade expansion there were a number of fringe subjects to be examined, such as transport facilities and the harmonization of standards. I was made responsible for a number of these subjects. Eckenstein, as I have said, was more of a visionary than an administrator. Consequently, not only was the mission badly planned, but the options and implications were also not fully thought through. The report was a poor one and achieved little other than to keep the subject warm. I benefited personally by considerably improving my knowledge of the three countries and of transport systems in Asia Minor.

At the end of the RCD mission I was invited to Bangkok for a liaison visit to ECAFE (the UN Economic Commission for Asia and the Far East), which had been pressing for support from UNCTAD. A trade division had been set up in Bangkok under the leadership of Prok Amranand, an able and energetic Thai with excellent royal connections, who later became Thai ambassador to the USA. This visit proved in retrospect to be more valuable than the RCD mission, and led to UNCTAD being asked to help establish an Asian clearing union. This was a job for a central banker, which I was not. I

was, however, able to start the process and then pass it on
to Dr Jorge Sol, a central banker from Salvador.

A follow-up visit to Bangkok in connection with the
Asian clearing union coincided with a visit by Gunal
Kansu from the UN centre for development planning in
New York, and Professor Austin Robinson of Cambridge
University. They were on an exploratory visit to examine
the possibility of setting up a project to help cooperation
in Southeast Asia, for which the Netherlands government
had provided a £500,000 fund.

The coincidence turned out to be extremely fortunate,
for UNCTAD was in a position to offer support and
expertise to such a project. We therefore drafted a
support project for UNCTAD, which also involved FAO
(the Food and Agriculture Organization of the United
Nations). The timing was opportune because the heads of
the five Southeast Asia governments (Malaysia, Singapore, Thailand, the Philippines and Indonesia), who all
spoke English, had recently met in Malaysia where they
played golf together. With the goodwill provided by the
golf they had signed an agreement to set up an organization for cooperation, and were in need of ideas to make
it effective: UNDP (United Nations Development Programme) funding of the project followed.

The papers for my Glasgow appointment were sent by
surface mail to Kenya and did not reach me within the six
months of my first UN contract. I therefore signed a
longer contract with the UN and spent the greater part of
the following three years working on the ASEAN project,

25. ASEAN, 1972.

for which a coordinating office was set up in Bangkok. Kansu was team leader with Robinson as adviser, and I was deputy team leader. Up to forty advisers and UN officials were involved in this project.

My personal responsibility was to coordinate the UNCTAD and FAO inputs into the project and to draft that part of the report concerned with trade policy. Robinson, working from a small hotel in the ski resort of St Cergue, in the Swiss Jura above Geneva, did the main drafting and overall coordination of the report. My eldest son acted as courier to bring the papers down to Geneva for typing each day as they were drafted. When the UN refused to pay for printing the report, Robinson had it printed in London and paid for it out of his own pocket.

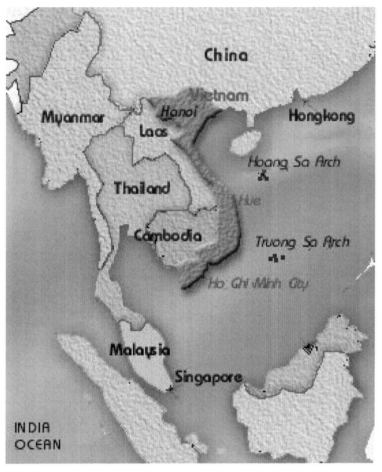

26. The ASEAN countries.

The ASEAN governments accepted most of the recommendations at a summit meeting in Bali in 1973. The UN
New York subsequently published the report as Issue No.
7 of the UN *Journal of Development Planning*.

Robinson was a very interesting colleague with whom
to work. He was an academic economic historian who at

the same time had an intuitive feeling for issues that mattered in government and administration. He understood the importance of scale and is, I think, the only economist who has written about the optimum size of countries (Kenya was I think near optimum size for efficient administration at the time of independence). In ASEAN he could see potential economies of scale in industry that he was hopeful of achieving. Yet, when I asked him about the importance of the EEC, he replied, not in terms of economies of scale but on the grounds that 'the member countries will never fight each other again.'

The success of the ASEAN project was largely due to having set up a UN team/ASEAN government coordinating committee at official working level. This met every six months while the team was collecting material and preparing recommendations. For each meeting the team would prepare a position paper and submit sectoral proposals that could be tried out on the committee. If the reaction was favourable the proposals were developed further for inclusion in the final report. If the reaction was unfavourable or hostile the proposals were dropped. As ASEAN had adopted a decentralized secretariat, which divided functions on a subject basis between the five governments, the meetings of the committee were held in each member country in turn.

This system worked very well and enabled everybody concerned to become acquainted personally at key operational levels, as well as to get to know the five countries

better. In retrospect, I think the ASEAN project was the
most successful piece of work I did for the UN. Years
later I took a study team of ECOWAS officials to visit
ASEAN. We breakfasted with Adam Malik, the then vice
president of Indonesia. I asked him what he felt was the
value of ASEAN to Indonesia. He replied, like Robinson
had about the EEC, 'We shall never fight each other
again.'

Towards the end of the ASEAN project I was asked to
participate in a mission to advise the island member
countries of the South Pacific Bureau for Economic
Cooperation (SPEC) about economic cooperation. This
was a most enjoyable mission to some delightfully
hospitable small countries. Very few of our recommendations were in the end adopted. The main reason was
that the economies of scale were very small, owing to the
small total populations of all the islands together.
Furthermore, the main benefits for each island came from
cooperating with a metropolitan country. Thus, for the
Cook Islands, there were major benefits in remaining
closely tied to New Zealand, which gave the islands
substantial financial and technical aid and to which they
could freely export their unemployed workers.

A French colleague in the mission with a Cartesian
approach to problems suggested we expand shark fishing
to alleviate the shortage of protein in the islands.
However, he failed to take into account that the local
sharks were viviparous, with a low reproduction rate, and
that the local fishermen disliked catching them. I

travelled to the South Pacific with him on a Quantas flight via Sydney. The French were unpopular in Australia at the time because they were exploding experimental atomic bombs in one of their Pacific island colonies, so when my colleague addressed an Australian cabin steward in French, the latter turned to me and said 'Can't you tell him to speak a language we all know, mate?'

Having arrived in Fiji, after an unsuccessful attempt to date an airline hostess, my colleague tried to phone his wife, but in view of the standoff with France had to get permission from the Fiji ministry of foreign affairs. This he duly obtained and he went to his hotel room to make the call. His wife was on holiday in the Riviera at the time in a house without a phone, so he had to phone her neighbour. After about a three-hour delay he eventually got through only to find that the neighbour was having lunch, which he refused to interrupt to call his wife, but agreed to inform her of his safe arrival. As my colleague had booked a personal call and did not get to speak to his wife, he fortunately did not have to pay for the call.

From Fiji, flying overnight in a small 146 jet across the International Date Line via Western Samoa, we went to Rarotonga in the Cook Islands . In Samoa big is beautiful, and when several rather heavy Samoan ladies boarded the plane the captain made us all get out to be weighed. We arrived in Rarotonga, which looked like a pearl in the ocean, early on Sunday morning to find that the customs officer was still in bed. However, the minister for education was at the airport and agreed to deputize for him. He asked if any of us had any whisky. This apparently was the only dutiable commodity. We were then garlanded by a hula-hula girl and accommodated in the government rest house, where the prime minister's daughter cooked us a steak breakfast.

Rarotonga was the nearest I have been to the Garden of Eden. It had an excellent free medical service and an almost empty hospital that New Zealand funded. A doctor toured the island daily and if you needed his services you left a white flag outside your front gate. Cabinet meetings were informal family gatherings over a morning cup of coffee, and on a Saturday afternoon I found the leader of the opposition down at the harbour repairing a boat with which he hoped to provide a service to attract the votes of the outer islanders.

On social occasions it was a woman's privilege to ask a man to dance, so, to avoid embarrassing her, a man would wear a flower above one ear if he had come with a wife or partner, but above the other if he was on his own. I went out to dinner with the Anglican bishop, but no one asked either of us to dance. Women danced a kind of hula-hula or shimmy, but the men were expected to do something more masculine. Male visitors who did not know this and imitated their partner by shimmying were a source of much local amusement.

In 1973 I carried out a mission to East and central Africa where I discussed the possibilities of assistance to the EAC, and advised the Ethiopian government on negotiations with the EEC for membership of the Lomé Convention. I also represented UNCTAD at the African Development Bank's annual meeting, and discussed collaboration in economic cooperation and regional integration work with the ECA and Lusaka subregional office. Ethiopia accepted my advice and joined the Lomé Convention. The discussions with the ECA and Lusaka suboffice were held with a view to developing plans for a trans-Africa highway, but these unfortunately never materialized.

Towards the end of 1973 I visited Liberia and Sierra Leone, two small Anglophone countries in a largely Francophone subregion, which, because they had cultural features in common, presented some interesting possibilities for cooperation. Both parties were enthusiastic about collaborating and the UN advisers on the spot were encouraging. The economies of scale would not be large, but it appeared that, combined with some cultural and educational cooperation, they might just be sufficient to justify setting up a formal cooperation scheme with a small secretariat. I therefore helped UN colleagues prepare a report that advised the establishment of a customs union of the two countries, to be called the Mano River Union after the name of the river that divided them geographically.

Our report was accepted with such enthusiasm that the proposed secretariat became a bandwagon onto which more and more people climbed. It became disproportionately large – an end in itself – and the more it grew the less efficient and more corrupt it became; so few of the hoped for advantages of cooperation materialized. Guinea joined the union, though linguistic and other difficulties meant that its participation amounted to little more than a token political gesture. The Liberian revolution, political strains between Liberia and Sierra Leone, and some incautious remarks in Sierra Leone about the new President Doe's wife, set the union back further.

In 1974 I became involved with my French colleague in cooperation work between Ghana and Upper Volta (now Burkina Faso), largely at the request of Robert Gardiner who had been executive secretary of ECA and who, as commissioner of planning in Ghana, was the only civilian in a military government. The two main areas for study were trade expansion in livestock and salt, and cooperation in developing the hydroelectric potential of the Black Volta River. As Upper Volta was landlocked, Ghana had significant transport cost advantages in exporting to Upper Volta, and in turn offered a ready market for livestock from Upper Volta. Unfortunately, there were continuing payment problems arising from the disastrous state of the post-Nkrumah Ghanaian economy, and the payment delays discouraged Voltain cattle traders from selling to Ghana.

In the reverse direction there was a market for Ghanaian salt, the comparative cost advantage of which was enhanced by some evasion of Upper Volta import duty by deft lorry loading, and under-invoicing by the salt manufacturer. Other Ghanaian manufactured goods tended only to appear in Upper Volta in the street markets, having obviously been smuggled in to avoid import duties and import controls, and to enable Ghanaian traders to acquire the fairly convertible CFA francs without having to hand them to their central bank. The language barrier, corruption, inefficiency and Ghanaian payment problems combined to act as an effective barrier to a significant increase in recorded trade.

Cooperation in the development of the Black Volta seemed a more hopeful possibility. Ghana had the Australian Snowy Mountain Authority prepare a technical report in English, and Upper Volta had *Electricité de France* prepare one in French. The practical issue was to agree on the sites on which to construct barrages for hydroelectric supply and irrigation.

A meeting was convened to try and agree on a first site. A delegation headed by a minister represented each country and, since both countries had military governments, in each case the minister was a junior military officer. After a day of discussions, with no retreat by either side, an impasse was reached. At the suggestion of the ambassadors accredited to each country, the reports were passed to them, to my French colleague and to me to study overnight. We found that both reports recommended the same site, but that each had given it a different name. The linguistic barrier had prevented this point being noticed.

We also tried unsuccessfully to do something to

improve communications between the two countries,
particularly by telephone. Apart from the minor incon-
venience of elephants pushing over telegraph poles, the
main problem appeared to arise from divided responsibility within the Ghanaian post and telegraph department. The branch responsible for domestic lines was not
responsible for trans-frontier lines and there appeared to
be little liaison between the two sections.

I was unimpressed by the Ghanaian P&T (posts and
telegraphs) department. A red letterbox at the International Hotel where I stayed had obviously not been
emptied for weeks because letters were almost falling out
of its opening. My colleague, who had at one time been
an inspector of weights and measures in France,
calculated that the box had not been emptied since the
trade fair two months earlier. In fact, most of the trade
fair correspondence was probably still in the box.

Through the desk clerk I persuaded the hotel manager
to ring the head postmaster of Accra to complain. He
thoughtfully asked why the box had not been emptied
and was told that it was 'because the lorry broke down'. I
had an appointment the next day with Robert Gardiner,
who was hoping that he might be able to use my report to
persuade the president to make some much needed
economic reforms. I told him about the overfull letterbox.
'Good God,' he said 'I am the chairman of the P&T
board.' He immediately went over to a telephone on the
other side of his office to tick off the head postmaster. His
own phone was out of order!

The most promising Ghanaian export to Upper Volta was undoubtedly salt, which, according to the import statistics of Upper Volta, had in the past been imported from Senegal and Egypt and only more recently from Ghana. Given that salt consumption is inelastic and does not vary from year to year, we were mystified by a sudden fall in Upper Volta's salt imports.

We decided to interview the proprietor of the Ghanaian firm that evaporated salt from the sea. He explained that the lorries carrying salt drove in a convoy of partially-loaded vehicles and, in the gap of several miles between the two frontier posts, half the lorries would offload their cargoes onto the remaining ones. These would then carry on into Upper Volta while the empty lorries returned to Ghana. As no customs officer would unload heavy bags of salt to count them, the salt was consequently under-declared and import duty paid on only about half the amount.

At our next meeting with Upper Volta's minister of finance, we drew his attention to the shortfall in the salt import statistics. When he sent for the commissioner of customs to ask for an explanation, the latter replied: 'We have a social problem at the frontier, Sir'.

In 1975, in addition to continuing to work on the Mano River Union and Ghana–Upper Volta project, my French colleague and I were asked to undertake exploratory missions to Rwanda and Burundi to advise on regional cooperation policies.

There were more visits to the Mano River Union and

Ghana–Upper Volta project the following year, and I now also began to cooperate with the International Civil Aviation Organization (ICAO) with a view to developing the kinds of air transport services that might encourage intra-African trade.

Our earlier missions in Rwanda and Burundi had led to these two countries establishing the Economic Community of the Great Lakes Countries (CEPGL) with Zaire. The most important tasks in the remit to this community were to support the joint development of the large methane deposits of Lake Kivu and the coordinated hydroelectric development of the region. German consultants had prepared a report on the Kivu deposits that showed there was enough methane to make nitrogenous fertilizers for all the coffee and tea estates in central and East Africa for many years to come. The local Belgian brewery had in fact used the methane for its power source. It was a very promising idea. Unfortunately, when Idi Amin seized power in Uganda, communications with the coast were interrupted, potential investors lost interest and the project fell into abeyance. I am confident that one day it will be revived.

In 1976 I took part in an UNCTAD mission to Bangladesh to advise on trade expansion and regional cooperation policies. The mission encountered a lot of red tape, particularly in the customs service, but it became clear that attempts to circumvent the red tape might affect the financial position of some officers. The mission also looked into the scope for cooperation with other developing countries in the production and marketing of tea, and in trade in pharmaceutical products.

In 1977 I visited Togo where an UNCTAD team was advising the government in the broad area of trade and economic cooperation. Here again there was a military government in power. It was headed by President Eyadema, whose name and photographs were plastered on posters throughout the capital, Lomé, along with slogans of support for him. Unfortunately, someone had inadvertently left out the letter 'r' on the posters, which were in French, so instead of stating that 'we will die for the president', they said that we are dying because of him!

At this time the Economic Community of West African States (ECOWAS) had just been set up formally under Nigeria's leadership and with ECA encouragement. Its membership comprised the 14 West African countries located between Nigeria and Mauritania. Over the following years it became my main advisory activity and I spent most of 1978 helping ECOWAS get started and preparing a report on its trade policy options.

The ECOWAS secretariat laboured under severe administrative handicaps. The accommodation in Lagos (in what had once been a government guesthouse) was cramped and unsuitable for the secretariat of a large group of countries. Spasmodic electricity supplies meant that we frequently had to work without electric typewriters, air conditioning or lighting; linguistic barriers limited verbal communication between Anglophone and

Francophone officials in the secretariat; and the combination of horrific Lagos traffic jams and poor security meant that even travelling to the airport could be a hazardous experience. The practice of holding meetings in different member countries meant that office equipment had sometimes to be moved by what amounted to a trans-Saharan safari. Under these difficult circumstances the executive secretary and his small staff did a very creditable job.

I was also asked to advise Cape Verde and Guinea-Bissau, both Lusophone countries, on mutual cooperation arrangements within the broader framework of ECOWAS. Both countries were extremely poor. Cape Verde was, however, well administered by highly competent officials and had provided middle-level administrators to other Portuguese colonies in the colonial days. Guinea-Bissau was not only poor but also short of educated officials. Its infrastructure was very basic. The local airline had only one aircraft, an old Dakota, and one pilot, so when the pilot got malaria the airline had to be grounded. My hotel in Bissau had no air conditioning, no food and no water; one woman from an international organization had a nervous breakdown and had to be evacuated. Some stalwart Russians on the ground floor solved their washing problem by carrying water in from a standpipe in the street. Food and drinking water had to be bought from a bar down the street from the hotel.

West Africa again took up most of my time in 1980, though I visited Rwanda and Burundi where, in addition to helping the secretariat of the CEPGL (*Communauté économique des pays des Grands Lacs*), I was asked to prepare a report on cooperation and commercial policies for the Kagera River Basin.

In 1980 I also went to Papua New Guinea where I was asked to advise on trade and cooperation policies in both regional and global contexts. This was a developing country rich in natural resources, with a basically sound economy. The main problem was to ensure a phased development programme, without incurring balance of payment problems and without wasting resources. I made a range of recommendations covering commodity marketing policies, development of shipping services, air freight rates, preferential trading arrangements, quarantine regulations, customs procedures, nomenclatures, and documentation, industrial standards, and industrial planning. But I have no idea if any were implemented.

At the end of 1980 a change in UNCTAD policy meant that my post of interregional adviser disappeared. ECOWAS work had, however, expanded and I was reassigned as senior adviser to ECOWAS, operating out of Geneva in view of the difficulties in working from Lagos. This I continued to do until my retirement in 1982. ECOWAS was a long-term operation with at least a ten-year time scale, and I did not feel I could see it through to completion, though I continued to do some work as a consultant until 1984. The first step was to ensure the cooperation of the different national customs departments. This was a difficult task in view of the different traditions and educational levels, the language and communication barriers, the all-pervasive problem of corruption, and the divergence of national interests.

It was clear that manual customs statistics were in many cases inefficient and often long in arrears. An early decision was therefore taken to use modern technology to computerize all the countries on a standard basis. Much time was therefore spent on standardizing nomenclatures and procedures. In view of its relatively high educational level we decided to make Cape Verde a front-runner in this operation. I wondered if ECOWAS might operate more efficiently with a decentralized secretariat along the lines of ASEAN and, to this end, I arranged a study tour of senior ECOWAS officials to ASEAN, but the idea was not adopted.

Looking back on my work with the UN, what stands out most is that success depends not only on the will of the countries concerned to cooperate, but also on their administrative capacity to do so. In Africa there was a large gap between stated intentions and the ability and will to implement them. This was not the case in Asia where, with one or two exceptions, national policy statements tended to err on the side of caution. This made it much easier to avoid excessive optimism, which leads to scepticism when there is a failure to match optimism with the delivery of results.

Three other points stand out. The first is that efficient national customs departments are essential to any scheme of regional cooperation. The second, an observation that

Arnold Toynbee had made, is that a common enemy or competitor provides a strong incentive for cooperation. In ASEAN this was a major factor in its early days. There was a need to present a common front to Japan, Australia, India and the EEC in trade negotiations, and there were at that time military threats from Vietnam and China. The third point is that there must be sufficient potential for economic gain from regional cooperation. This was manifestly not the case in the South Pacific where greater economic advantages were to be gained from cooperation with a developed country or group of such countries.

13

Epilogue

LOOKING BACK ON my life I am fascinated by the way in which chance, albeit it alternated with some appropriate decision-making, has shaped my life. I never planned my career. It just happened through a combination of chance events and opportunistic choices. Had I not wanted to learn to drive and joined the gunner section of the OTC, I might never have had the chance to go to India. Had an ex-footballer not been court-martialled my military career might have been very different. Had I not met T. Ngulthong Paita I might never have got a mention in dispatches and my first promotion. Had the Japanese not wrong-footed General Giffard I would never have been flown into Imphal. Had I not come across small mechanical calculators in Calcutta I would never have thought of the rapid method of calculating army rations and staff loading tables that may well have contributed to my further promotion. Had I not been made to write with my right hand in my kindergarten, would I have been posted to Turkana and would June have written the biography of Leslie Whitehouse, *Jomo's Jailor*?

27. Oliver and June, Watlington, 1997.

While this book was being prepared for publication the 2007/8 Kenya elections had just taken place and the whole world is facing what may be an economic and monetary crisis that could perhaps be comparable with that of the 1930s. I have also just finished reading Martin Meredith's masterly book, *The State of Africa: A History of Fifty Years of Independence.*

It is tempting to look back and ask why is Asia progressing so much faster than Europe and the USA? And why has Africa made so little economic progress since the onset of independence fifty years ago? Africa's natural resources are no less bountiful than those of Asia.

People have little control over some determinants of economic progress, such as natural resources, climate and genetics, but they do control the political and economic spheres, infrastructural development, law and order and religious beliefs and practices. The British Empire grew because Britain encouraged technological advances, military leadership, financial innovation, wide use of the English language and good administration. It ended when Britain became militarily and financially exhausted. The USA has dominated the world since the Second World War. It has benefited from the English language, and world technical leadership. Its dominance is now ending in a mixture of financial mismanagement and military over-spending.

The Association of South East Asian Nations (ASEAN) has been a success story. Starting with five members it now has ten member states, most of which are showing considerable economic growth. It includes a wide range of religions; English is the common working language; and its systems of government include monarchies, republics and military dictatorships. They are fortunate to have a wide range of natural resources and good levels of rainfall. The group has a decentralized administration. The member countries show political wisdom and good political judgement, and they have remembered Vice President Adam Malik's wise words that 'We will never fight each other again.'

In the Pacific, the Pacific Islands Forum has expanded from the original seven members of SPEC (South Pacific Economic Cooperation) to sixteen members, and with two associate members. Its working language is English, though the two associate members are French speaking. There is no fighting between the member countries and

Christianity is the majority religion. They share a wide range of natural resources. However, with a few notable exceptions such as Botswana, African countries, and groups of African countries, have either made very little progress, or even tottered on the brink of collapse.

The East African Community has acquired two new members, Rwanda and Burundi, but it no longer has a single currency, and it has lost many common services. English is the working language, though Swahili is also widely spoken. It has made little progress with trade preferences. There are potential benefits from greater cooperation in transport, trade, manufacturing, energy planning and research. But progress is likely to be slow until there is more stability in the member states. If the southern Sudan were to become an independent state it could well join the East African Community.

The Economic Community of the Great Lakes (CEPGL) is still in existence but is hamstrung by poor communications and the virtual collapse of administration in Zaire. Its potential for developing the methane resources of Lake Kivu, communication and transport facilities, and the energy resources of the region seems certain however to ensure its survival and revival some day.

In West Africa, Cape Verde has left the Economic Community of West African States (ECOWAS) to form an association with the European Union. ECOWAS *per se* has made little progress, though it provided a military force (ECOMOG) to help stabilize both Sierra Leone and

Liberia. There is considerable room to improve transport and communications, but limited potential for expanding trade, other than on a bilateral basis between coastal and landlocked states. ECOWAS could learn from ASEAN about how to use collective bargaining power in international trade negotiations on behalf of its member states.

In Kenya a closely-fought election with some vote rigging by all parties led to a political deadlock and a near breakdown of law and order, with very serious results both for the Kenya economy and for that of its regional neighbours. International peacemakers have brokered a deal between the parties, for all concerned have too much to lose from continuing disturbances. But unless the underlying problems are tackled the Kenya economy will remain precariously balanced.

One of these problems is what a German anthropologist, Gunnar Heinson, describes as 'security demographics' and the theory of the 'youth bulge'. His theory is that once the proportion of males in a country between the ages of 15 and 29 reaches 30 per cent, it is more likely to dissolve into civil war or start a conflict with its neighbours. After the recent rioting in Kenya Heinsohn pointed out that the Kenya population has grown by a factor of 13 since 1928, and that 15–29 year-old males now represent almost exactly 30 per cent of the population. A similarly dangerous situation is now developing in Uganda.[2]

2. See Sam Knight, 'Births of a Nation', *Financial Times Magazine*, London, 1 March 2008, pp. 14–21.

For stronger economies than African ones, in America or Asia the 'youth bulge' need not be a problem. Youth unemployment in the USA actually fell during the 1960s despite a flood of job-seekers from the enormous postwar baby boom generation. Likewise, growth rates across Asia have managed to outstrip the growth in the labour force, in China comfortably so. But in sub-Saharan Africa and parts of the Middle East in the same period, average GDP growth has been virtually cancelled by the growth in the labour force.

The root problem is a population that is growing so rapidly that it prevents growth in per capita incomes even when the economy is growing overall. In the years after independence Kenya had an annual growth in GDP of nearly 8 per cent a year. The resultant prosperity led to a population explosion and a rate of population growth of over 4 per cent a year, which the actuaries said was impossible. The inevitable results of over-population are tribal friction, competition for available land and a drift to the towns, with a growth in urban slums and a large number of young males with too much energy and no visible source of income. They start criminal gangs like the Mungiki, with robbery, traffic hold-ups, and in pastoral areas, cattle raiding.

The population and land problem in Kenya is aggravated not only by tribal divisions but by racial divisions between the Nilotes, Bantus, Nilo-Hamites and Hamites. These are as great, if not greater, than the racial divisions in Europe, where 1500 years have elapsed since the break-up of the Roman Empire. With education and development these divisions will become less important, but it will take time to eradicate them. Even in Britain today there can be fighting between young Scots, Welsh, Irish and English males, if only at rugby matches.

The second major problem in Kenya is the mis-allocation of economic resources through corruption, which reached a peak with the Goldenberg scandal during President Moi's period in office. When President Kibaki was elected he promised to stop corruption, but he has clearly failed to carry out that promise.

Kenya has the great advantage of a relatively free press and some outspoken leaders who have condemned corruption. Unfortunately, the attitude of most Kenya politicians and senior civil servants seems to be that 'everyone has to eat'. Though there are some who are not corrupt, it will not be easy to get a change in this attitude.

There was little or no corruption in Kenya in the early years of independence when there was a high rate of economic growth. How and why did corruption grow? As secretary of the first official public inquiry into corruption in Kenya, the 1967 Maize Commission of Inquiry, and a senior treasury official, I was in a good position to see the change happening.

There was almost no corruption in the colonial administration. There were several reasons for this. Civil servants were paid an adequate though not excessive salary with pensions on retirement. Any civil servant found guilty of corruption would not only be dismissed but would lose his pension. He would also be socially ostracized for 'letting down the side' and would have to resign from his clubs. This moral sanction was supported by a legal sanction 'the Code of Pecuniary Interest'. This code prevented a civil servant going into business and laid down what presents he could or could not accept. It was thrown out of the window in 1971 when the government accepted the Ndegwa report (Report of the Commission of Inquiry (Public Service Structure and Remuneration) 1970–71), which recommended that civil servants should be allowed to have business interests.

In a country where there is no old age pension, loyalty to the extended family is greater than loyalty to the state, for security in old age and help during periods of unemployment become the responsibility of the extended family. This means that successful politicians and civil servants are under great pressures to help their less successful relatives, and accepting bribes is an easy way out. In colonial times we tried to start a national provident fund, a small initiative to help the elderly in Kenya, but greedy hands plundered its investments during President Moi's term of office.

It is tempting to blame capitalism and Sessional Paper no. 10 for Kenya's problems. However, Tanzania's experience of corruption and failed economic management under President Nyerere, who was incorruptible, showed conclusively that nationalization and public ownership is not the answer to corruption in East Africa, and only leads to gross economic mismanagement. The problem is to make capitalism work more efficiently under Kenyan conditions.

Several measures could help this process. The first is constitutional reform to introduce a more equitable geographical distribution of the benefits of government. President Kenyatta was wise enough to see this. His balance was unfortunately upset by several events, of which the most important was the cold war when Vice President Oginga Odinga backed the East and lost his place in the cabinet. The second is to restore the code of pecuniary interest, or something similar, and make it applicable to all civil servants, and to force ministers to declare their business interests and directorships.

A third measure the government might explore is the possibility of introducing a more African approach to the problem of corruption, to look into whether traditional African oaths could in some places and circumstances be adapted when swearing in officials and ministers on taking office.

The fourth measure is to ensure that government wages and salaries are index linked to inflation. The fifth is to revive the National Provident Fund. The sixth would be some lengthy prison sentences for ministers and senior officials found guilty of corruption, to show that the government is serious about stopping it.

Nothing would give me more satisfaction, 40 years after the first commission of inquiry into corruption in Kenya, than to see Kenya leading the way in the reduction of corruption in Africa.

Appendix
Summary of Movements
1940–46

1940–1941	
20 December– 31 January	At Willems Barracks Aldershot
1941 4 January– 13 February	On board HT *Highland Chieftain* (1 January sailed from Clyde; 24 January Freetown; 11–12 February Durban)
13 February–3 March	On board HT *Windsor Castle* (22–24 February Mombasa; 3 March Bombay)
8 March–10 June	At officers' training school, Bangalore
11–13 June	Hotel Majestic, Bombay
14–16 June	Laurie's Hotel, Agra
17–18 June	Hotel Cecil, Delhi
21 June– 20 September	At RIASC school, Kakul, NWFP
20 September–4 October	34 SIS, 7 Indian division Batrasi camp, NWFP
4 October	Moved to Attock Fort and promoted captain
29 October–14 November	On a course at the Camouflage school, Kirkee, Poona
1–4 November	Giving evidence to a court martial at Kakul

14–25 November	Back at Attock Fort
28–30 November	To Wah and Calcutta to embark for Rangoon
5 December 1941	Posted to 54 SIS, at Campbellpur, Punjab
1942 1–11 January	On ammunition recognition course at Rawalpindi arsenal
11–22 February	On leave in Delhi and Jaipur
20 March	Arrived Lohardaga, Bihar with 54 SIS and joined 14 Indian Division
4–15 April	14 Indian division moves by road and river boat to Comilla, East Bengal via Dhanabad, Burdwan, Barrackpore, Goalundo Ghat, Daulatganj
16 April	54 SIS moves to Laksam Junction and joins 49 Indian brigade
7 May	49 brigade moves by rail to Dimapur (Manipur Road)
11–13 May	49 brigade moves by road to Manipur state (Palel) passing through Imphal just after its first bombing by the Japanese
13 May–10 August	In field hospital at Imphal with malaria
1–13 September	Near Palel
14 September	49 brigade moves up to front line positions on the India–Burma saddle and in the Kabaw valley. 54 SIS camped in Dead Mule Gulch
1 November	49 brigade relieved and moved back to Imphal
15 November	Left Imphal to go on senior officers' course at Kakul
3 December	Arrived Kakul
1943 17 January	Left Kakul

23 January	Promoted to major as a DADS and arrived at HQ 33 Indian corps at Pedur camp, Vanyambadi, South Arcot district, Madras presidency
1–28 February	On exercise Trump 1, visited Tiruvannamalai and met Sri Maharashi Ramana. Visited Madras, Salem and Trichinopoly
4–23 April	On leave in Ootacamund, Nilgiris and Mysore
May	On exercise Fog around Pillur, Madanapalle and Kolar goldfields
June	On exercise Tippoo around Ranipet, Madanapalle and Kolar
July	On exercise Trump 2 in the Tiruppatur gap with 19 and 25 Indian divisions
2–12 September	On leave in Ootacamund with Philip Heale
6–16 October	On leave at Choyis hotel Cannanore visiting Mahe, and Telicherry
22–28 October	By train to Delhi i/c 33 corps baggage party
29 October	Arrived Delhi and joined HQ Rear Army HQ SEA as a DADS
1944	
24 March	Flown by Dakota to Imphal to join HQ 4 corps as DADS for air supply
26 March–26 June	In the siege of Imphal
7 July	Left Imphal and returned to Delhi via Comilla
14 July	Back at Rear Army HQ SEA in Delhi
24 August– 10 September	On leave in Gulmarg, Kashmir with Philip Heale
16–30 September	In hospital in Delhi with jaundice
1–16 October	Sick leave in Naini Tal
27 November	HQ ALFSEA moved to Barrackpore near Calcutta

1945

12–15 June	Visit by air to HQ 12 Army in Rangoon, Burma
23–30 June	On leave in Shillong, Assam with Philip Heale
15 July	Arrived Rangoon by sea and appointed DADS 12 Army
28 July	Promoted to lieutenant colonel and appointed ADS 12 Army
11–26 November	On tour to Toungoo, Meiktila and Mandalay, combined with a short leave at Maymyo

1946

1 January	HQ 12 Army becomes HQ Burma Command
12 March	Proceed on leave by air to Calcutta via Akyab, continuing by rail to Kalimpong
23 March–10 April	On trek to Tibet via the Jelep La pass to Yatung and Pharijong returning via the Nathu La pass to Gangtok, Sikkim
12–13 April	At the Himalayan Hotel, Kalimpong
14–21 April	At Spences Hotel, Calcutta
25 April	Back in Rangoon
13–18 July	On tour by jeep to Pegu, Sittang, Martaban and Moulmein
26 July	Leave HQ Burma Command and enter transit camp
29 July	Embark on HT *Carthage* from Rangoon calling at Colombo (3 August), Suez (11 August)
21 August	Arrive Tilbury
22 August	Discharged from the army
October	Returned to Oxford University.

Bibliography

Habeler, Gottfried von, *Prosperity and Depression* (League of Nations, Geneva, 1939)

Hazlewood, Arthur, *African Integration and Disintegration* (RIIA, Oxford, 1967)

Kenya Government, *Sessional Paper no. 10 on African Socialism* (Government Printer, Nairobi, 1965)

Knowles, Oliver, 'Some Modern Adaptations of Customary Law in the Settlement of Matrimomial Disputes in the Luo, Kisii, and Kuria Tribes of South Nyanza, *Journal of African Administration* (London, January 1956)

Knowles, Oliver, *Planning the Receipt of Aid* (Cambridge Overseas Studies Committee, 1962)

Loynes, J. B., *From Currency Board to Central Bank* (Economics Club of Kenya, 1963)

Macdonald, David, *Twenty Years in Tibet: Intimate Experiences of the Closed Land among all Classes of People from the Highest to the Lowest* (Cosmo Publishing, New Dehli, 1996)

Macdonald, David, *Touring in Sikkim and Tibet* (AES, New Delhi, 1999)

McCann, John, *Return to Kohima* (McCann, Oldham, 1993)

Maize Commission of Inquiry, *Report of the Maize Commission of Inquiry* (Government Printer, Nairobi, 1997)

Ndegwa, Duncan, *Walking in Kenyatta Struggles* (Kenya Leadership Institute, Nairobi, 2006)

Ndegwa, Philip, *The Common Market and Development in East Africa* (East African Institute of Social Research, Makerere, Uganda, 1965)

Robinson, Ronald, *African Development Planning* (Cambridge Overseas Studies Committee, 1963)

Robinson, Ronald, *Overcoming Constraints to Development* (Cambridge Overseas Studies Committee 1965)

Robson, Peter, *Economic Integration in West Africa* (Allen & Unwin, London, 1983)

UNCTAD, Report of the UN Inter-disciplinary Mission to Review the Scope for Inter-regional and International Cooperation between Sierra Leone and Liberia (UNCTAD/TE/65, Geneva, 1973)

Report of the UN Preliminary Mission to the South Pacific Bureau for Economic Cooperation (UNCTAD/TE/70, Geneva, 1974)

Trade Expansion and Economic Cooperation between Ghana and Upper Volta (UNCTAD/TE/84, Geneva, 1975)

Le Developpement du Kivu et la cooperation economique regionale (UNCTAD/TE/114, Geneva, 1976)

United Nations, Report of a UN Team on Member Countries of the Association of South East Asian Nations, *Journal of Development Planning*, no. 7, UN, New York, 1974)

Watkins, Elizabeth, *Jomo's Jailor: Grand Warrior of Kenya* (Britwell Books, Watlington, 1996)

Watkins, Elizabeth, *Oscar from Africa* (Radcliffe Press, London, 1995)

Watkins, Elizabeth, *Olga in Kenya: Repressing the Irrepressible* (Pen Press Publishers Ltd, London, 2005)

Watkins, Elizabeth, *Cypher Officer* (Pen Press Publishers Ltd, Brighton, 2008)

Index